OUR HIS...

By OXFORDSHIRE GUIDES

THE FIRST FIFTY YEARS, 1910 TO 1960

© Una M Dean & The Oxfordshire Guide Association 1999
British Library Cataloguing in Publication Data
A Record for this book is available from the British Library
ISBN 0 9537002 0 8

Repro by Ford Graphics, Ringwood, Hants.
Printed by The Witney Press, Witney, Oxon.

Published by The Oxfordshire Guide Association
World distribution by The Oakwood Press (Usk), P.O. Box 13, Usk, Mon., NP15 1YS,
or locally from the author 01865-779855
E-Mail: oakwood-press@dial.pipex.com
Website: http://ds.dial.pipex.com/oakwood-press

Foreword

Many people have contributed items in this volume which gives a glimpse of how it was in the Girl Guides Association in Oxfordshire from 1910 -1960, how much it has altered and what remarkable women there have been who have worked so hard for the girls in their care.

The Association has seen so many changes and every aspect has altered since the beginning, from the uniform that was worn, the Promise that was taken (even, today, dropping the word "girl" out of the title) to the attitudes that govern the weekly meetings and activities. All this is reflected in Guiding in Oxfordshire.

The idea to compile this story was put into action a number of years ago and it is to the great credit of the editor and her research team that it has been completed.

A very big thank you goes to everybody involved. Most remarkably all the work has been done for free, from the postage, paper and telephone calls to the travelling and hours of research. The team wanted to do this as another contribution to an Association that means so much to many.

I hope that you, the reader holding this book, will find interest, inspiration, admiration and pleasure from the history contained within it.

Vivien Pleydell-Bouverie
(County Commissioner 1983 -1991)

2nd East Oxford Guides' Registration Certificate.

3rd Headington Guides, 1922.

Acknowledgements

I wish to thank the History Committee for their hard work in researching material for this book and for their support and encouragement to me in the task of writing it. Joyce Crowther-Hunt is our Chairman, the members are: Mary Boulton; Eileen Hawkes; Gwyneth Jenkins; the late Beryl McVicar and Joyce Winston. I acknowledge the trust placed in me by the County Executive in putting up the money to publish this book. I owe thanks to Maureen Chatterton for meticulous proof-reading, to Rodney Deval for processing the photographs, to the late Rosalie Brown for art work, to Janet Lane (née Titchmarsh) for permission to use her work, to the three County Commissioners who have encouraged us, Vivien Pleydell-Bouverie, Vivienne Scouse and Evelyn Walker. Special thanks to Jane and Ian Kennedy and Oakwood Press for help and advice on publishing. Thank you to everyone who has sent in photographs, memories, anecdotes, encouragement and interest. I wish to acknowledge the extracts I have taken from Jackson's Oxford Journal, the Oxford Mail, the Oxford Times and from Guiding publications.

Any profit from this book will go to the Oxfordshire Guide Association, to help with the re-building of Jubilee House.

I must make it clear that this book is my work, the views expressed are mine alone and I am responsible for any errors or omissions. I trust I have not offended anyone, if I have it was entirely unintentional and I apologise.

Una M Dean (Mrs)
Oxford
1999

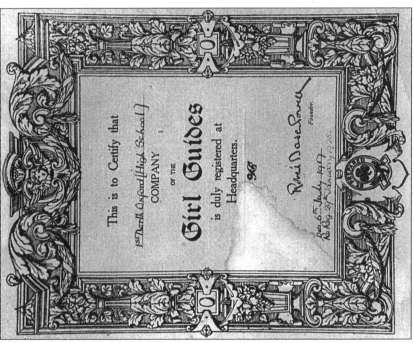

Above: *Registration certificate signed by B-P, 1917.*

Left: *Hilda Jeffs, c1912. She died aged 14.*

How Guiding Began

Major General Robert Baden-Powell, hero of the siege of Mafeking, wrote a book based on his army experiences. He called it *Scouting For Boys*. In 1909 he organised a camp on Brownsea Island in Dorset for boys from London and the camp was run as the book advised. It was an enormous success and soon boys were forming themselves into groups and calling themselves Scouts.

In 1910 a rally was held at Crystal Palace for the Scouts and inevitably some girls turned up. They called themselves Girl Scouts and wore a hotch potch of uniforms, most of them had a stave and a wide-brimmed hat. Baden-Powell was pretty desperate about these girls and he asked his elder sister Agnes to organise them into Girl Guides. This she did and she was our first president. Guiding grew and flourished and gradually it spread through the world.

When Baden-Powell married he asked his wife to take over the Guides which she did with enormous success. She was popular, she had common sense and she had a way with the girls. She remained our Chief until her death in 1977.

As time went on Rosebuds/Brownies were organised, Rangers and, much later, the Rainbows. The Movement was based on Faith but not a particular faith. All races, all creeds and all colours are accepted without question into the Guides (and the Scouts).

This book attempts to trace the history of Guiding in the County of Oxfordshire for the first fifty years - from the time it all began to 1960. A second book is on the stocks, the second fifty years.

Dresses which Brownies might wear. The first should be either brown or blue; the second and third blue; and the fourth brown. Nos. 3 and 4 are suggested as being the best.

Brownie dress suggestions.

1912, Scout register used for Guides.

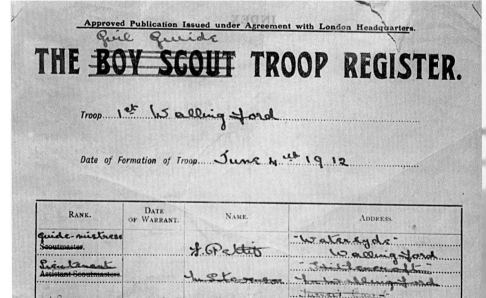

In the Beginning

The first authenticated record of girls in Oxfordshire wanting to join the new Movement sparked off by the book *Aids to Scouting*, published in 1900 by the then Major General Baden-Powell, comes in the Scout County Executive Committee minutes of May 1909. The committee refused an application from the Vicar of Headington for recognition for a patrol of Girl Scouts. It is however highly likely that unrecognised and unofficial patrols of girls were within the County by this date. On 27th July 1910 Jackson's Oxford Journal (weekly local paper) reports:

Since the Guide Movement first originated many have swollen its ranks. We believe that there are about 60 in the Oxford Region.

A photograph shows Guides practising semaphore signalling and ambulance duty on Shotover Plain. In 1911 the first County Commissioner for Oxfordshire was appointed, Mrs Sanderson Furniss, whose address was 4 Montague Street, Russell Square, London.

It is interesting to find that in 1912 a register in use for a Guide Unit had a printed front page reading: *THE BOY SCOUT REGISTER*, with *BOY SCOUT* crossed through in ink and the words *GIRL GUIDE* hand written above.

A Guide leader in the County introduced us to her grandmother who in 1913, when she was eight years old, became a Rosebud. Rosebuds were the fore-runners of Brownies. They were not recorded at C.H.Q. (neither were Girl Scouts) which makes it difficult to find out about them. The meetings our Rosebud attended were in the kitchen of a hall in Polstead Road, Oxford. The leader was an infant school teacher. They did not wear uniform and they had 'talks on life'. Grandmother later joined a twelve-member Girl Scout troop which also met in Polstead Road, in 1916.

This unit was registered as 1st Oxford. There were Rosebuds and Girl Scouts elsewhere in the County by this time.

In 1914 the 1st Henley-on-Thames YWCA Guide Company opened and it was registered on 13th April 1915. There were three other units in the area but only 1st Henley has a continuous record to the present day.

It is difficult to say which units were first as in the beginning units were numbered 1st Oxford, 2nd Oxford but were later re-registered in geographical areas. For example: 2nd Oxford, registered in October 1915 became 4th East Oxford later; 12th Oxford (GFS) Guides, registered in May 1918, and Brownies, registered in November 1919, were re-registered as 1st East Oxford (GFS) Guides and Brownies in January 1925. Similarly the 13th Oxford (CWL) Company (June 1920) became 2nd East Oxford (CWL) Company in 1924. The Cowley BBB became 5th Cowley (Church Army) Company in 1945 and then became 5th Cowley (St Luke's) in 1957. This re-registering took place all over the County and it is sometimes difficult to make the right connections.

It would seem that existing groups of girls changed themselves into Guides and Brownies, the Girls' Friendly Society and the Catholic Women's League being examples. The Better Britain Brigade, or BBB, seems to have been formed under the auspices of the Church Army to encourage children to be positive about their country.

In June 1914 Miss Baden-Powell, then President of the Guide Movement, brought her unit, Pinkleys Green, Maidenhead, (the first unit to be registered), to demonstrate drill to 1st Oxford and Stanton St John Companies.

In 1915 the Henley Y.W.C.A. company and 1st Woodstock were registered; in 1916 1st Oxford appeared (the unit our Rosebud joined as a Girl Scout); 1917, 1st Witney and 1st Chipping Norton (Town) Brownies and 1st Chipping Norton

(Church) Brownies; also in 1917, 1st Headington Rangers were registered, 1st Headington (Quarry) Guides, were re-registered, 7th Oxford re-registered as 1st North Oxford, (Oxford High School Company) and 8th Oxford became 1st West Oxford; in 1918, 1st Wheatley, 2nd Headington and 1st Charlbury Guides were registered. From this random selection of early units it seems that Guiding sprang up in all parts of the County simultaneously, groups of girls formed themselves into patrols of Girl Scouts and persuaded adults to lead them - registration came later. The flood of registrations continued - in 1920, 1st Warborough Brownies and 1st Ewelme Guides; in 1921, 1st West Oxford Rangers and 1st Goring Guides . . . and so on.

The local paper reported on 15th March 1916:

Miss Baden, who is President of the Girl Guides, visited Oxford and presented badges to various companies of the local Girl Guides at the Institute, Polstead Road.

Also in 1916 Sir Robert and Lady Baden-Powell inspected Boy Scouts and Girl Guides on the lawn at 163 Woodstock Road, the home of Professor Thompson. Over one hundred Scouts and Guides were present.

In 1916 Guides in Woodstock gave an entertainment to raise money for the Red Cross Society and for a hut for soldiers at the Front - World War 1.

July 1917 saw a rally at St Hugh's College where Viscountess Harcourt witnessed a Guide display. The Red Cross received £14 from Woodstock Guides after a dance in the Town Hall in Woodstock. July 1918 and there was a Girl Guide display at Kingham. Chipping Norton, Idbury, Charlbury, Churchill and Kingham Guides took part.

It seems that Guiding was very active in its formative years, these are just a representative sample of all the activities in Oxford publicised in the local paper or the Guide Magazine.

5

In 1918 1st Chipping Norton Church Brownies, newly registered, formed a Guard of Honour for Princess Mary in Queen's College Gardens on the Princess' 21st birthday. A detailed log-book from 3rd Headington Guide Company gives an interesting picture of the beginnings of that particular unit. GFS stands for Girls' Friendly Society, a Church group.

1918 January 22

Mrs Burrows (Division Commissioner for Oxford) and Miss Stephens (Division Secretary) came to Highfeld by Miss Singer's invitation and spoke at a GFS meeting on the Girl Guide Movement. Miss Singer hoped to start a GFS Company shortly.

February 25

Miss Doyne (County Secretary for Oxfordshire) came to a GFS meeting and explained more about the Guide Movement and how to start a Company.

March

During March those girls who wished to become Guides came several times to Miss Singer's house where they learnt the Guide Laws and were taught knots etc. Miss Constance Russell, who was training to be Lieutenant, took them for drill etc.

April 4

Miss Doyne examined the girls for their Tenderfoot test, when nearly all passed.

April 23

Miss Singer took the girls for the first time to their new Headquarters in the old Mission Room in Church Street, where they cleaned the room and tidied the garden.

April 30

The girls met at HQ and finished tidying the garden.

May 2

The girls went and had games. Miss Singer brought their new uniforms to be tried on.

May 14

Miss Stephens enrolled the first 14 Guides at Headquarters, when Miss Doyne, Miss Singer, Miss Fairfax Taylor, Canon and Mrs Colson were present. Canon Colson consented to be Chaplain to the new Company which was registered as the 3rd Headington GFS Company.

The Company consisted of 2 Patrols, the Blackbird Patrol and the Canary Patrol. . . .

May 16

A GFS Associates meeting was held at which Miss Singer gave an account of the new Company and it was arranged that it should meet every Tuesday and Thursday at 6.30pm.

The log book goes on to give an account of activities which includes, on 10th September 1918, digging the potatoes they had grown in the Guide garden and taking them to the Wingfield Hospital (Nuffield Orthopaedic Centre). In October it was reported that a severe epidemic of influenza prevented regular attendance at parades. On 11th November 1918 the Guides paraded at the Thanksgiving Service for the Armistice - the actual day the First War ended. The entry for 28th December 1918 reads:

The end of their first year found the Company flourishing but unfortunately tending to get slightly out of hand owing to lack of proper officers.

The log book continues with many interesting pieces - on 15th May 1919 the Guides went bluebell picking and Miss Singer took the flowers to a poor London parish; at a County Rally in July 1920 the four Headington Companies built a bridge which was inspected by the Chief Guide, she wrote a letter of thanks to them; great emphasis is placed on training for both girls and adults. From 1921 there were regular camps.

This is to ⎯⎯⎯ Certify that

Winifred Wilson

has been Enrolled a B·P Girl Guide

I trust you on your honour, at all times to do your best to carry out your Duty, and to do a good turn to some body every day.

Agnes Baden-Powell

Above: *Certificate signed by Miss Agnes B-P.*

Left: *Uniforms, around WW1.*

Below: *Armistice Badge.*

I was not allowed to join the Scouts - Dad and Ma did not want me to be a soldier. At first Scouts seemed very military, B-P was a soldier of some repute, the saviour of Mafeking, it seemed that Scouts were soldiers in the making.

I joined the Guides in about 1915 or 16. I was not allowed to go to camp - too unladylike. I did not expect Mother to allow me to join, she was very insistent on the ladylike aspect of life. I suppose I nagged her into submission and I expect Pop supported me.

Father took us to Crystal Palace, when we saw the Girl Scouts following the Boy Scouts, we wanted to join. I knocked on the Officer's door and asked if I could be a cruet. I meant recruit, of course.

A girl came down the drive on her bicycle with all kinds of things dangling from it, she told us she was a Girl Scout looking for Accidents or Good Turns and had with her everything she thought might be useful, 1st Aid box, rope, frying pan, etc, etc. I was fascinated.

3rd Oxford Guides and Brownies, 1919.

These figures come from Oxfordshire County Annual Reports:

1917/18 - there were 326 Guides in Oxfordshire.
1919/20 -
36 Companies, 519 Guides; 172 Brownies; 46 Rangers.
1920/21 -
15 Commissioners, 142 Guiders, 8 Secretaries;
60 Companies, 980 Guides; 23 Packs, 30 Brownies.
1921/22 -
13 Commissioners,132 Guiders,10 Secretaries;
69 Companies, 1,048 Guides; 26 Packs, 382 Brownies;
7 Ranger Companies, 72 Rangers; 0 Cadets.
1922/23 -
15 Commissioners, 161 Guiders, 10 Secretaries;
74 Companies, 1,255 Guides; 37 Packs, 477 Brownies;
13 Ranger & 2 Cadet Companies, 134 Rangers.
1923/24 -
16 Commissioners, 170 Guiders, 14 Secretaries;
86 Companies, 1,362 Guides; 40 Packs, 571 Brownies;
15 Ranger & 1 Cadet Companies, 135 Rangers; 3 Cadets.
1924/25 -
16 Commissioners, 185 Guiders, 19 Secretaries;
79 Companies, 1,239 Guides; 39 Packs, 546 Brownies;
20 Ranger & 2 Cadet Companies, 233 Rangers; 20 Cadets;
1 Post & 2 Lone Companies, 5 Post & 15 Lone Guides.

The 1999 Census figures were as follows:
777 Commissioners & Guiders;
91 Companies, 1,540 Guides; 194 Packs, 3,752 Brownies;
70 Rainbow units, 856 Rainbows;
12 Ranger units, 197 Rangers and Young Leaders.

Miss Faith Doyne, Headington Quarry. *East Oxford Guide.*

BP Guide Badge.

Guiding Grows in Oxfordshire

On the 28th July 1920 - Oxford Girl Guides held a rally on Worcester College Football Ground. Lady Baden-Powell inspected the troops, supported by the Mayor and other guests. Jackson's Oxford Journal (weekly paper) reported that Lady Baden-Powell took the salute *'accompanied by her staff officers'*. There was a gymnastic display and a bridge building display at which Headington excelled.

During the 1920s Lady Baden-Powell came to Oxford, and addressed members of the Movement in the Town Hall. Brownies sat in the hall, Guides and Rangers on the balconies. One lady who was a Brownie at the time reports: *The Chief Guide started by saying: "you can all stand up and have a jolly good wiggle" - so we did!*

On 13th May 1921 the 9thA Oxford (Savemake Glove) was registered. In March 1927 the Captain of this company was Miss B W Smith of 44 Wellington Square, Oxford. The glove factory was in one of the roads off the Botley Road, a building later used by PO Telephones. At that time workers were younger and Guides were older, hence a unit in a factory.

November's Guide Magazine in 1921 reports:

In spite of the only rain which fell during August falling upon our Camp, the 1st Banbury, Adderbury and Wroxton Companies had a most successful and enjoyable four days under canvas at Sibford during the first week in August.

This camp used the Sibford Quaker School premises to put on a very successful concert. It is recorded the local Vicar inspired the Guides at his camp service. Miss Fairfax, Captain of 1st Banbury was the Camp Commandant.

The Guide published on 23rd April 1921 carried the following: *The visit to Oxford of Princess Mary, our President, on Friday March 11th had been looked forward to with both pleasure and anxiety, and, when the day broke bright and clear, great was the gratitude of the lucky ones in our twenty-three Guide Companies who had been chosen to form a Guard of Honour for Her Royal Highness. In accordance with the Princess's wishes, and by kind permission of the Principal, Miss Penrose, the Guard was posted in the beautiful grounds of Somerville College. Before arriving at Somerville the Princess was presented with a boquet [sic] by the High School Company of Guides.*

The Guard of Honour was 70 strong, consisted of 50 Guides (two from each Company) and 20 Guiders, under the command of the Senior District Commissioner (Mrs S Montague Burrows). The County Commissioner (the Hon. Mrs North) was unfortunately unable, owing to illness, to be present. The Royal Salute was given, and two District Commissioners and the District Captain were presented. The Princess then inspected the Guard; nothing seems to escape her eye, and many hearts were gladdened by the kindly attention she paid to the badges that told of good work. She asked that each Guider should be presented to her and had a cleverly chosen word for each. The Queen had watched most of the inspection, and when a little later we gave three hearty cheers for Her Majesty and the Princess, they were smilingly received.

So - by April 1921 we had at least twenty three official Guide Companies in the County and an assortment of Commissioners and even a District Captain - and an unknown number of unregistered units.

Jackson's Oxford Journal reports:

A bouquet of pink tulips and freesias was handed to Princess Mary by Miss Barbara Wright supported by two other Guides, Miss Joy Holmes and Miss Ursula Joachim.

Such formality in the newspaper.

14

The *Guide* of 18th June 1921 said:

A most successful Operetta, entitled "Pearl the Fishermaiden", as given by the 1st Bloxham Company ... All the parts were splendidly played ... very great credit to those who had coached them (Miss Ommanney, Captain, and Miss Chipperfield, Lieutenant) ...

Also in 1921 *The Guide* reported:

The Dedication of the Guides' Colours took place in Deddington Church on Whit Sunday, when the Guides and Brownies paraded in full numbers under the leadership of their Captain, Lieutenant, and Brown Owl ... address ... spoke of the symbolizm [sic] which a flag represents and of the inspiration to comradeship and loyalty for which it should stand ... District Commissioner ... impressing on the Girl Guides the special need there is in these days for good citizenship and loyal service to our Country and Empire ...

On 20th August 1921 *The Guide* carried this report:

A Rally of the South Oxfordshire Guides was held at Joyce Grove on Saturday, June 25th by the kindness of Mrs Fleming OBE, District Commissioner for Watlington ... winning Company - the 2nd Henley.

From the list of those present at the Rally it seems that Miss Doyne was County secretary and Miss Houle her assistant. Miss Faith Doyne was Captain of 1st Headington (Quarry) Guides and Miss Houle was her Lieutenant. The Oxford Eye Hospital was founded by Miss Doyne's uncle and there is still Doyne Ward. At the Rally were County Commissioner, Mrs North and her Staff Captain, Miss North.

The Guide of 10th September 1921 writes of a Girl Guide Rally for North Oxon which was held in Wroxton Park in July. Wroxton won the cup with 3rd Banbury and Adderbury Company joint second. These rallies appear to have been the same, with Mrs and Miss North attending and the Guides cooking dinner over an open fire as part of the competition.

1st Warborough Guides, 1921.

Oxford Guides, 1923. Are they wearing camp overalls of the time?

On the 17th September of the same year another Rally was reported, this time for Mid-Oxfordshire. The winning Company was 1st Headington; second was the John Correy Company, 2nd Chipping Norton; third was the Northleigh Company. A later entry in the *Guide* says that 1st Headington won 'Premier honours' at this Rally.

The Guide of 24th September 1921, about 1st Ewelme:

... a delightful display was given by the Guides and Brownies, in aid of Company funds on July 23rd, in Ewelme Manor garden. The programme consisted of Indian club exercises, skipping, signalling, duologue, very well acted by a Guider and a small Guide. It is difficult to say whether the performers or the audience enjoyed themselves most. Nearly £5 was realised for the Funds.

The Guide on 8th October 1921 reports on Wallingford:

A Patrol Leaders' Conference was held on June 18 at the house of Mrs Llewellyn, the District Commissioner. All Companies in the district sent their Patrol Leaders and a Patrol Leader from Oxford came over and presided. The Patrol Leaders read papers and debated on, "Are girls as brave as boys", and "Should the swimming test be compulsory for First Class". Games were played after the debates, and everybody left after a good tea, voting the meeting a great success.

The Guide 18th February 1922:

Oxford - On Thursday, December 13th, the 2nd Oxford Guides held a concert ... in aid of camp funds for next Summer. The programme included 'cello and piano solos, songs, dancing, and a Guide play involving signalling, ambulance, and stretcher drill. In the interval a competiton for guessing the weight of a cake was held with the cake ... as the prize. The amount raised was £2 0s 8d, which, as no one in the audience could have spent more than 11d [less than 5p] in the course of the evening (including admission, programme, and the maximum of three guesses for the cake) and a large number, being children,

17

can only have paid 2d, shows that the audience was a large one. .... the Company will be able to be under canvas for longer than the weekend, which was all that was possible this year.

The Guide 18th March 1922:

The 1st Ewelme Guides and Brownies gave an entertainment of Tableaux Vivants on January 14th ... about £12 was realized for the funds.

The Guide 1st April 1922:

The 1st Thame Company and Brownie Pack held a most successful joint entertainment on Thursday, January 5th: the hall was packed and the audience was a most appreciative one ... over £8 was taken to swell Company funds.

These extracts show that Guiding was alive and well throughout the County and fund raising was as necessary then as it is now.

In 1922 Adderbury Guides camped in Eynsham Park but numbers were low due to an outbreak of measles. It is so easy to forget that illnesses which are now wiped out, or from which present day children are protected, were much feared killers just a few years ago.

In 1923 1st Adderbury Guides gained full marks for the dinner of stew and fruit in the District Cup competition and later that year camped at Brightstone, Isle of Wight, it was such rough weather that the Colours could not be flown.

The Great Adventure, 1933. Unfortunately the occasion is not clear and I do not know the author.

There were special celebrations in Rome ... decided that a British contingent of Rangers should go, ... On August 28th 113 Rangers and officers caught the boat train from Victoria. There were 5 from Oxford, I was one of 3 from 7th North Oxford Rangers, a Tawny Owl and a lieutenant. As it was unusual for ordinary people to go abroad ... a large number of friends and relatives came to see us off from Oxford ...

The train to Folkestone had open carriages and when looking along all the arm rests had navy blue elbows. We changed trains in Paris and travelled through the night. ... no sleepers in 3rd Class, ... wooden slatted seats like park benches. ... We were given breakfast in a big railway hall on the Italian border, ... a message from the Chief Guide wishing us safe journey and God speed. What a cheer went up! ... a special meeting with the Pope ... in the Vatican. We stood round the walls so that he could see us all, he walked round reading our name tapes and as he read Oxford his face lit up, aah yes, he had been to Oxford as a student. We were pleased, good old Oxford! ... In one of the large Basilicas, [as we were] marching in rows of four, very orderly, a man came up to me and asked who we were. Guiding and Scouting had been suppressed .... under Mussolini and people were curious ... The long journeys cut into our holiday time but we saw many of the sights of Rome and we would not have missed it for the world.

In the 1920s members of the Mitford family were active in Guiding in the Burford area, providing District secretaries and Commissioners. They were the family of 'Honourables' immortalised in Nancy Mitford's books and included the tragic Unity Mitford. This Mitford link with Guiding has continued.

3rd Headington Guides at Lee-on-Solent, 1924.

3rd Headington Guides setting off for Foxlease from a camp at Niton on the Isle of Wight, 1920.

Steeple Aston Flower Show, 1922.

World Camp, Foxlease, 1924

The present unsatisfactory condition in the world ... we have internal warfare of class against class and party against party ... similarly the Churches agree to disagree on minor points of form ... Women ... take their place ... in the government of the country. They are the recognised advisers of the men ... have the ... influence over the characters and future lives of their ... sons. ... we in the Scouts and Guides have our opportunity for doing a great human good not only in our own several countries, but, if we act in co-operation, for the world.

The words above ring true today, they are taken from the Chief Scout's Welcome to the delegates to the 1924 World Camp, at Foxlease, a time when the Great War was a powerful memory. Lord Baden-Powell's words are printed in a delightful book 'The World Camp 1924'.

The Camp Chief was Mrs Janson Potts, District Commmissioner, South Oxford. Mrs Janson Potts was presented with the Silver Fish Award at the end of the Camp *'for good work in the Movement for many years culminating in her excellent organisation of the World Camp, in the capacity of Camp Chief.'* (quote from the Book).

The Oxfordshire sub-camp commandant was Miss Davidson from Sussex, aided by QM, Miss Fairfax, from Oxford and Equipment Manager, Miss Staveley, also Oxford. One of the PL orderlies of the Olympus Camp (explanation in a minute) was N. Sheard from Oxford and R. Sargent, Oxon, is listed as a PL attending the camp.

The sub-camps were in the grounds of Foxlease. Surrey organised two sub-camps, one of them was 'Olympus' and was for the overseas Commissioners for whom no room could be found in the house. There were 22 Commissioners in Olympus from 17 Dominions and foreign countries plus the

3rd Headington Guides at Minehead, 1921.

1st Wallingford Guides waiting for the Queen Mother (Queen Mary).

Chief Guide. These ladies were jokingly referred to as Olympians early in the camp's planning, it stuck and Olympus became the official name of their camp.

Four patrols of selected PLs did the general work in the twenty five tent camp of Olympus, in addition, each patrol was responsible for the care of a group of Olympians. The girls referred to their charges as 'Goddesses'. The Chief Guide had two orderlies a day, thus the maximum number of girls had a turn. The orderlies ate first, in a big marquee, and then served 45 to 50 adults. The camp provided for those sleeping in the Cottage and The Link.

There is a wonderful piece in the book about the Camp Hospital, it is reprinted from 'The Nursing Mirror'. There was a woman doctor, two trained nurses, one of whom was called home during the camp; orderlies of Guides with Sick Nurse or First Aid badges or with special nursing skills. There was a ward plus outpatients and visitors. Minor illnesses reported morning and evening, serious cases received a tent visit before being moved to the hospital. The article says only four to five beds were occupied at any one time, chiefly septic tonsillitis. There was a case of rheumatism, one of slight fever, one appendicitis, one gastritis, one of nervous exhaustion. (It does not say if the latter were girl or adult!)

Any hysterical or nervous case was isolated in the hospital for twenty-four hours. This proved to be a most satisfactory way of dealing with this condition, which, however, one is proud to say, was almost non-existent in our Camp.

Minor cases were cuts, bites and sprains, - no broken bones. Just over one hundred cases were seen, ~10% of the campers. Minor things must have been self-treated.

Messages received included one from The Chief Guide which stated that the suggestion of a World Jamboree such as the Scouts had held was undesirable for girls and a friendly happy gathering was preferable. The President of the Girl

Right: *Mrs Janson Potts Camp Chief and also South Oxford District Commissioner.*

Below: *The camp water cart, cartoon from camp book.*

Guides of the British Empire, The Princess Mary, whose wedding present money had endowed Foxlease, and Mrs Archbold who had given the house to the Movement both sent messages. *(The book on the World Camp calls the lady Mrs Archbold, we were always taught Mrs Archbold Storrow.)* The arrangements for the camp seem primitive to our eyes: bedding transported on a truck affair on bicycle wheels; girls in full uniform and brimmed hats at all times; milk dippered from a churn; the greengrocer with a hand cart; the canteen cart and the water cart were horse drawn. I could go on ... There were over a thousand campers, about 200 very large loaves and up to 116 gallons of milk were used daily [1 gallon = 8 pints]; the meat wagon brought 70 joints at a time. Distributing food at the start was strenuous; keeping up with the camp's daily orders was tricky; coping with the bits and pieces that remained was a nightmare.

And the whole camp was presided over by an Oxford Guider.

'My Goddess is still asleep; shall I wake her?'

(Cartoon from camp book)

" So this is England !!"

W.V.H.

Above: *Unknown campers.*

Right: *3rd Headington off to Church Parade from camp at Eynsham, 1923.*

The following event was also in 1924, please note that it was the Scout Jamboree from which the Chiefs were returning.

MEETING THE CHIEFS

Returning from a hike with my Guide Patrol, belonging to the 2nd Witney Company, we met Lord & Lady Baden-Powell along the Northleigh-Witney road. They were having an overnight visit to stay with our District Commissioner at Eynsham Hall. The car stopped and we all had a hand-shake and a chat after we had given them a smart salute! The Chiefs were on a country wide tour after they had left the Scouts' World Jamboree.

It was a very happy and excited patrol who returned home tired after their 7 mile adventure.

Maud confesses she was told the Chiefs would be on that road at that time, I wonder if the Chiefs were pre-warned?

In 1925 the 1st Adderbury Guides won a District Competition and the following is an extract of the report of the results:

77% Good all round Company. Marks would have been even higher but for weakness in Legends and Inspection. This last was chiefly a matter of details. Points were lost for ends of cotton, spots on tunics, dirty lanyards and name tapes, etc. Trees - good in both sections; Rules of Health - good; Morse - good; Gadget - good idea well made; Lashings - neat. Second bar at the bottom would have been good to hold plates.

In April 1925 there was a 5thA Oxford Guide Company, they are reported as giving an entertainment in the Summertown Congregational Hall. Eynsham Guides received special permission from Sir J M Barrie to perform 'Kiss for Cinderella' at Eynsham Hall. In June Lady de Trafford inspected the dinner at Deddington Girl Guide rally which was held at North Aston. A photograph shows that the dinner was on the ground so presumably it was camp cooking.

The Princess Royal came to Oxford to receive a cheque for £6,924 in aid of the Benevolent & Orphans Fund of the NUT

1st Headington Guides, led by Miss Houle, while camping at Minehead in the 1920s - presumably going to Church.

Headington Guides in camp, 1925 & 1929.

(National Union of Teachers), Guides formed a Guard of Honour for her outside the Town Hall - in pouring rain.

In July of 1925 the Chief Guide, Lady Baden-Powell, opened the Oxfordshire Girl Guide Rally and fete at New College cricket ground. At this time there were an estimated 1,400 enrolled Girl Guides and Rangers in the County. At the time of the Rally Lady Burrows was CC; Mrs Janson Potts and Mrs Miller were Division Commissioners; Miss Houle was Secretary and Miss Pemberton her assistant. The Oxford Times report says of these ladies:

... on whom the brunt of the general arrangements devolved and whose tact and courtesy contributed in no small degree to the smoothness and success with which the whole afternoon's programme was carried through...

The Chief Guide's Standard, which had been worked by the County Commissioners of the British Isles, was carried and escorted by three PLs who had represented Oxfordshire at the World camp at Foxlease the previous year. Included amongst the VIPs are:

the Hon Mrs de Beaumont (CC, Cambridgeshire, representing the sister University); Miss D C Mellor (County Secretary, Birmingham); Major Edmondson, MP and Mrs Edmondson; Captain Henderson, MP and Mrs Henderson.

The Chief Guide's speech was cheered and applauded, below is a summary of the paper's lengthy report of the speech.

The Chief felt that people thought that Guides looked nice but did not always realise the training that lay underneath. Parents did not want their daughters to be tomboys and some thought that Guides were not quite the thing. For the last nine or so years the Movement had been growing without a great fuss and was proving itself. Its aim was to train young girls to develop themselves to be useful, loyal, honourable, capable and helpful so they might become better mothers and home makers. There was no wish to take the girls away from their parents, teachers or pastors but to give them useful training in their spare time. The Movement had grown from nothing to about half a million members and slowly people were understanding that there was something in it all. The rally would help those present to see what the girls were doing and whether the Movement was helping the girls mentally, morally and physically. Worldwide there were over 30 nations with Scouts and Guides. Young people were being trained to think, not only for themselves, but of others and thus the Movement would make for a better international understanding. It was unfortunate that not enough adults were coming forward to lead the girls. The Chief Guide thought that tennis, boating, dancing and having a good time did not do much good, whereas in the 'finest game there ever was' women and girls could be doing some good for other people.

The afternoon's programme followed the usual pattern of tent-pitching and displays plus entertainments. Handcrafts were on display and for sale, 1st South Oxford Rangers had made and fitted a beautiful doll's house. The Local Associations had a produce stall in charge of Miss Feilden and Miss Rawnsley; the Scouts helped at the gate; music was by the Oxford and Bucks Light Infantry; First Aid was by the Red Cross, fortunately hardly used.

After a march past the competition results were announced, the winner of the County Shield was:

3rd North Oxford (St Michael's) with 91 marks;

there followed:	4th South Oxford, 84½;
1st Whitchurch Gate and	
Goring Heath, 83;	1st Woodstock, 82;
2nd South Oxford, 81½;	2nd Headington, 80½;
1st East Oxford, 65½;	1st Swalcliffe, 63½;
1st Adderbury, 61;	1st Harpsden, 59.

Above: *Friends, 1925.*

Right: *Miss Houle 2nd Headington.*

Below: *Patrol and six emblems.*

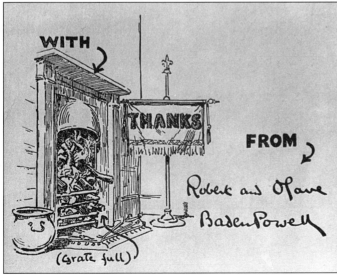

(Grate full)

Robert and Olave
Baden Powell

Above: *Headington
Guides at
Zeebrugge, 1929.*

Left: *Thank you
card from the
Chiefs, received by
1st Witney, 1929.
[Note the grate-full
by the fireplace.]*

South & West Oxford Guides in camp, Bridport, 1928.

Lady Baden-Powell closed the rally saying how impressed she was by the County's Guides - as good as she had seen anywhere in England - jolly, flourishing and keen.

Lady Baden-Powell also visited the Wingfield Hospital (now the Nuffield Orthopaedic Centre) and met long-stay patients who were in the hospital Guide Company.

An interesting wedding took place in this year (1925) at SS Mary and John Church in East Oxford, the bride, the groom and all the attendants wore Guide and Scout uniform and there was a uniformed Guard of Honour.

Guides attended a special Church Parade, wearing black armbands on their uniforms, when Queen Alexandra, wife of Edward VII and great-grandmother of our Queen, died.

A 'This is Your Life' for Mrs Alice Beale reveals:

You [Alice] joined the Brownies in 1925 ... walked, every week, from Benson to Ewelme for your Brownie meeting, going past Cottesmore Farm ... one evening ... the cows were coming in to be milked just as you and your friends were passing. The other girls ran quickly past but you were very frightened of cows and stood, rooted to the spot. You simply could not move and your friends ran on ahead. There were a great many cows and they ambled slowly into the farmyard while you stood hopping from one foot to the other, too frightened to cut through them but so worried about being late for Brownies that, in the end, it all became too much for you and, yes, you wetted your knickers!!

Later Alice's kipper kedgeree became a legend in Benson camping circles. Alice is in the Trefoil Guild at Benson at the time of writing this.

The Headington Quarry Company, with Miss Doyne, camped in Belgium in 1926, they stood on the mole at Zeebrugge, where a great battle occurrred in The Great War.

The following quote was given by an elderly lady who spoke with great enthusiasm about her Guiding days:

I was 14 when I first joined the Girl Guides - that would be 1927. I would have joined earlier but my stepmother did not let us join anything. When I finished school (at 14) I was given the post of Monitress [Pupil Teacher] and that entailed going to Night School and one evening to Guides. The Guide meeting was the highlight of the week, I was able to get my own uniform, which included a navy blue hat with a very large brim which we ironed with sugar and water to keep stiff. They were really hideous but we were very proud to wear them. The meetings were very businesslike and we had to behave ourselves. There was great competition between patrols, particularly about the gaining of badges, it was working for badges that gave us most satisfaction. One in particular that I remember was the Bird Watcher's Badge and to help us in this was Father Leo O'Hea, a keen Ornithologist. He used to take us to Wytham Woods, Brasenose Lane, along the banks of rivers etc, he knew the names of all the birds and where to find the rarer species. We got our badges. We camped a weekend at Kirtlington Park. One time my friend and I decided to play a joke on the Company. The hall at St Aloysius School was divided by a screen and we used the room furthest from the door. To liven up the meeting, Molly was to put a sheet over her head and come in when we were all assembled, put out the lights and I would say to Captain, "I will go and put them on." The sight of Molly with a white sheet over her head reduced me to hysterics, much to the consternation of Captain and the rest of the Company.

In 1927 the Kidmore End log book reports attendance at a County Competition, there was Folk singing and Ambulance work. The same year the company camped near Rye and the camp was *'washed-out'*.

The first mention of the University Scout and Guide Club is in 1929.

I remember we used to camp on the Squire's rabbit warren.
[Marcham near Abingdon]

The Duke of Marlborough's game keeper did not believe my story of practising stalking and tracking ready to teach my Guides. He tied me to a tree and went off to ask the Duke about me. I was pretty cross!

My first Guide hat had a very wide brim and a chin strap. We had to iron the brim while it was very damp. It was like a wooden board! Sometimes we used a sugar and water rinse before ironing and then it had a gloss as well.

I did not know which way up was which for the Union Jack. The books said put the widest white stripe at the top. 'Which side?' I asked myself, 'against the pole or the loose edge?' Here was I, starting a Guide Company, and I could not even fly my own flag. Eventually I took my courage in both hands and made a guess and got it right.

Oxford High School Company, 1932 and 1934.

Leading to War

In the early 1930s a Company at St John's, Banbury, was started by a Miss Jessie Bird. This is based on memory, there is no record, maybe it was never registered. The ladies who remember talk of camps at Lord North's at Wroxton Abbey. The St John's Parish Centenary book names Miss Bird as starting Brownies there. Unfortunately a fire at Miss Bird's home destroyed her records and photographs. It was not unusual, at this time, for a Guider to commute by bicycle from camp in Broughton Castle grounds to work in Banbury.

Guide and Scout Weekend

In the official programme the occasion was announced as Oxfordshire Boy Scouts & Girl Guides but the 3rd Headington Rangers put us first in their log. This weekend was also recorded in the Kidmore End Log Book.

A weekend was planned over 1st - 4th May 1930, to coincide with a visit from the Chief Scout and Chief Guide to Oxfordshire on 1st May.

The foreword from the programme of events was written by the two County Commissioners, Sir Montague and Lady Burrows. *The Chief Scout and Chief Guide are paying us a very great honour by coming among us for a whole day on May 1st. We are but a small place and they generally have to reserve themselves nowadays for very large gatherings. It is the more important therefore that we should show ourselves worthy. How shall we do it? By our discipline, our smartness, our enthusiasm; by our desire to help others rather than push ourselves forward; by our determination not to grumble at small annoyances or little errors which are often unavoidable*

West Oxford Guides in camp, Minehead, 1933.

and always unintentional; in short, by our team spirit, the spirit of the Jamboree. We shall be under the eye of the public, too, both City and University - a further reason for not lowering such reputation as we may have acquired already; and we sincerely hope that those members of the public who are not already interested in, or connected with, the Movement will come to the afternoon meeting and hear our Chiefs and judge for themselves whether we deserve their support. Our watchwords are brotherhood, service to others, international friendship, peace and goodwill, respect for religion and law; and we venture to hope that while nations are struggling with their greater difficulties, we, in our lesser way, have been, and shall be, allowed to do something for the rising generation, on whom, after all, everything depends.

The first day, Thursday 1st May, saw a public meeting, in the Oxford Town Hall at 3 pm, chaired by the Chairman of the County Council, at which the two Chiefs spoke. Tickets for the limited seating were free but there was a silver collection. At 7.30 pm on the same day, also in the Town Hall, there was to be a County Rally of Rangers, Rovers, Guides, Scouts, Brownies and Cubs, *public not admitted*. In the event two separate Rallies had to be held, one for the boys and one for the girls, because of the demand.

The two Commissioners and two Chiefs spoke and there was a sing-song. On Friday there were three showings of the World Jamboree Film, The Guide Film and Cubs Courageous, in the Corn Exchange, George Street, Oxford. The 2.30 pm performance was reserved for country Scouts and Guides and the public; 5.15 pm for Cubs and Brownies with the ratio of 1 adult to 10 children, (compulsory); 7.45 pm was for the City Rovers and Rangers, Scouts and Guides. The cost was 6d per person, 4d for Cubs and Brownies, with a few reserved gallery seats for adults at each performance [12d = 1/- = 5p].

41

Joyce Winstone, 1930 She tucked in her tie as it 'flapped about' and she wanted to be smart.

Alice Beal of Benson as a Brownie.

Brownie Guiders' Warrant Badges.

Saturday saw a Grand Palaver in the grounds of the Radcliffe Observatory and the public was *cordially invited to attend.* It began at 3 pm with a March Past followed by a Wheel of Life. The rather faded newspaper pictures show large circles of Guides and Scouts holding ropes to link them together, moving round in opposite directions. A ring was either all Guides or all Scouts. Next came teas for visitors, 1/- [= 5p], and folk dancing. This was followed by displays, exhibitions of handicraft, which were for sale, side shows, a produce stall and the Observatory Tower was open at 6d a time. This included: *... an unparalleled view of Oxford and inspection of [a] unique collection of Ancient Astronomical Instruments.* There was a camp fire and then dancing on the lawn for 6d. It was scheduled to end at 10 pm. The proceeds went to Oxford City Boy Scout and Girl Guide funds.

On Sunday there was a Service of Thanksgiving in the Sheldonian Theatre with a collection for the Wingfield Orthopaedic Hospital, now the Nuffield Orthopaedic Centre. The 3rd Headington Ranger log shows that the whole weekend was a great success and greatly enjoyed by the girls. Unfortunately the hand writing is difficult and equally unfortunately, the newspaper cuttings are too faded to reproduce. I give a few quotations from the log:

The happening of this most eventful Week End ... this was the first and great day - County Day when the Chiefs came to Oxford. All the Company's parents were invited to the public meeting ... the Town Hall was full ... the Chief Scout was presented with a Golden Arrow from the Scouts and Guides ... evening ... 2,000 Rangers, Guides and Brownies ... there was a sing-song and both Chiefs spoke and had a tremendous reception ... Silver Fish to Lady Burrows ... after this the Scouts and Cubs had their Rally, also about 2,000 strong ... six of the company ... Guard of Honour ... First Class and All Round Cords. The Jamboree and Guide films ... most of the company were able to get to the 7.30 performance. The day of the Grand Palaver ... after a wet morning it cleared just in time ... the afternoon was lovely ... March Past of over 2000. The last day came all too soon ... enjoyed the mass Service in the Sheldonian.

The newspaper reports that enormous public response created the need for an overflow meeting on the Thursday afternoon. The Golden Arrow, made of gilded oak, according to the paper, was engraved with the City and University Arms, the arrow was the symbol of the Jamboree.

From the Oxford Mail:

Those who sneer at the Scout movement and decry it as of no value should have gone to Oxford Town Hall last night ... So great was the demand for accommodation that the carefully prepared plans of the organisers went astray and instead of holding one rally, as was originally intended, two separate events had to take place.

From the Oxford Mail description of the Thanksgiving Service:

The Sheldonian Theatre, Oxford, has been the scene of many impressive gatherings but I have never seen a more wonderful gathering than that which took place in the historic building yesterday afternoon, when the Scouts and Guides of Oxfordshire held a Thanksgiving Service.

... hundreds of boys and girls ... in their picturesque uniforms and gaily coloured scarves, crowded into the tiers of seats and the galleries were decorated with troop and company colours. ... stood the choir who led the unaccompanied singing ... this was one of the most striking features of the afternoon ... 'Jerusalem' and 'He who would valiant be' were sung in a such a way as only children can sing ... I felt sorry for the large crowd which could not gain admittance ... content to ... listen to a choir of nearly 1,000 voices.

From the address by Rev P Leonard:

The Scout and Guide Movement is like a sheet of stamps, each Scout and Guide is like one of the stamps which, although retaining its individuality, is joined together at dozens of different points. ... The glory of a stamp is not its colour or its design but the fact that is a great servant ...

The Mail refers to crippled Guides and Scouts being brought to the Service from the Wingfield Hospital NOC [Nuffield Orthopaedic Centre] by Rover Scouts. They were pushed on flat, wicker, bath chairs - a long walk for the Rover Scouts. There is a great deal more, all complimentary, the Week End was obviously a roaring success. One cannot help but regret the passing of this level of public interest in our Movement.

Alma Hall

Alma Hall is situated in Alma Place, off the Cowley Road near the Plain. Alma Place degenerates into a foot path which links through to St Clements, one side of this path is Alma Hall. It is a brick-built building with a kitchen, storage space and a main hall. In 1933 it was purchased by the then East Oxford District which was approximately the area now occupied by City 1. Gradually, as Guiding became more concentrated, the original geographically large districts were broken down to smaller areas which meant that by the late 40s, early 50s Alma Hall belonged to a District of about 6 units. 2nd and 4th East Guides and Brownies met there as did District meeting, AGMs, LA meetings, etc and District camping gear was stored there. Later the District became smaller as slum areas in St Clements were cleared and evacuees returned home, some unwillingly, and the hall was not used very much. By the 1960s Alma Hall was no longer used for Guides and it was rented out to a Chinese gentleman. There was endless trouble with the place. It was decided, grudgingly in some quarters, that the ownership of Alma Hall should revert to its original area, namely City 1 Division. The Division Commissioner of the time reports

South Oxford Guides in camp, 1931.

opening her front door to two smartly suited gentlemen who had come to take away property to the value of a new manhole cover in Alma Place, a manhole cover reputedly the responsibility of the owners of Alma Hall. Eventually I convinced them that it was not down to me, the tenant had not informed me of the problem with the Council, that I did not own Alma Hall personally. It was quite scary, they were bailiffs and had enormous powers. My husband was not amused. That problem was sorted out. Alma Hall was sold and the money went to Division 1. Some of it was used to bolster the Jubilee House Building Fund, in the form of a loan and a gift. East Oxford District's camp equipment became homeless and the Division paid for storage.

In January 1933 the Hall was the venue of the LA meeting, at which a report was read by Mrs Teal, District Captain.

All the companies seemed quite happy and making progress with 2nd Class and Badge Work. ...Some had attended week-end camps at Kirtlington Park ... some ... camp for a fortnight. 50 Guides had attended the league of Nations Service in the Sheldonian Theatre. The 1st East Company were second in the Division Hike and Tracking Competition. [City Division - all the city.] In December the Guides made and filled stockings for poor children in Risca and on December 9th a trail was held ...

The Brownie report was read by Miss Massey.

... They seemed to have had very exciting outings to Bagley Woods etc and some had been to the Kidlington Zoo. One Pack had cooked a sausage supper which was incorrectly eaten out of the frying pan.

1934 saw a cross-country signalling chain, a sort of Chinese Whispers in Morse. The recipient was the Chief Guide.

In 1935 South Division was registered, it included Goring District and Henley District, both registered in 1922. This was the origin of the present Chiltern Division. Also in 1935 Lord and Lady B-P attended 1st Henley's 21st birthday party.

South Oxford Guides at Beckley, 1932.

1st Witney Rangers, both taken for the Silver Jubilees, 1935.

2nd South Oxford, Camp Campden, 1930.

In January 1935 the City Division Minutes [City, one Division] gives suggestions for training officers. Between 22nd January and 19th March there were to be eight trainings involving fourteen sessions. Four of these sessions were Moral Education Talks. Later the Minutes report that an average attendance of 25 Officers was achieved as the trainings on Woodcraft and Camp were very well attended.

... The question of training for the Division was to be brought up in the Autumn and Commissioners were to find out from their Guiders what the feelings on the subject really were.

The City were expecting a visit from 250 Rangers from Birmingham, volunteers were required to show the visitors round Oxford.

There was a National Service in St George's Chapel, Windsor in June 1935, to celebrate King George V's Silver Jubilee, there was a contingent from the County including a Guide from 4th West Oxford (St Barnabas) and a Ranger from Cowley. There was a Division Service in the Cathedral. Guides attended the Scout Beacon Fire on Jubilee Day.

Two articles in the Oxford Times report on a County Rally. Another gives no unit name but refers to South Oxfordshire:

The Company has recently gained 7 Sick-Nurses, 6 Child Nurse and 2 Cook's badges. We have also had much practice in bedmaking and bell-tent pitching as we were chosen to represent S. Oxon Division at the County Rally, ... Other displays were ridge-tent pitching, erection of flagstaff, badge demonstrations, 'good turns', games, folk-dancing and a model Camp. We are looking forward to Camp at ... Brading, I.o.W. ... shall be pleased to see our friends either on Visitor's Day ... August 12th or any other day. We very gratefully acknowledge 5/2d [26p] from the Jubilee Day Sports Committee to our funds and which we shall use to help Guides to come to Camp. D.F.W.

5th East Oxford Guides, 1936.

Map Reader and Emergency Helper badges.

Pioneer Badges and Primrose Patrol Emblem.

Right: Miss Wells, 1938.

4th Cowley Brownies.

The other article shows that Guiding was held in very high esteem in the County. It begins thus:

GIRL GUIDE RALLY OXFORDSHIRE ASSOCIATION'S FINE DISPLAY.

The important work which the Girl Guide movement is carrying out in catering for the mental, moral and physical training of young girls was clearly demonstrated on Saturday afternoon in South Park, Headington, when the Annual County rally of the Oxfordshire Girl Guide Association took place in the presence of a large crowd of the general public. Over 1,000 Guides from all parts of the City and County contributed to an interesting programme, which should serve to arouse great local interest in the movement. ... Nearly all the companies in the County were represented and the programme was carried through with great success.

The rally was opened by the Duchess of Marlborough and those present included Lady Evelyn Mason (County Commissioner), Lady Saye and Sele (President of the County Association), Lord Saye and Sele, the Hon. Geoffrey Fiennes, Lady Burrows (the former County Commissioner), the Mayor and Mayoress of Oxford (Coun. and Mrs G. C. Pipkin), Mrs G. Herbert Morrell (who lent the Park), Lord and Lady Elton, Miss Browning (HQ Training Dept.), Capt. the Hon. Bertram Mitford (High Sheriff of the County), Mrs Early and Mrs Slater-Harrison (vice-presidents of the Association), Major Burrows, Col. S. Jervis (County Scout Commissioner), Mr L. Soanes (City Scout Commissioner and Major A. Caccia (County Scout Secretary).

The article goes on to say that the Duchess and the official party walked to the platform through a Guard of Honour of Guides with their company standards and there was a concerted rush into the arena of the Brownies and Guides, into a horse-shoe formation.

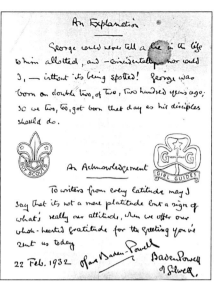

Translation:

An Explanation

George would never tell a lie in the life
to him allotted, and - coincidentally - nor would
I, - without its being spotted! George was
born on double two, of two, two hundred years ago,
so we two, too, got born that day as his disciples
should do.

An Acknowledgement

To writers from every latitude may I
say that its not a mere platitude but a sign of
what's really one's attitude, when we offer our
whole-hearted gratitude for the greeting you've
sent us today.

22 Feb. 1932

[Signed Olave Baden-Powell , Baden-Powell of Gilwell.]

The Duchess, in declaring the rally open, said she deemed it an honour to be present, especially as she herself had been a Girl Guide. A great deal of good was being done in the country by the movement, which was teaching young girls to be loyal to God and to the King ...

After breaking the Union Flag and the World Flag there was a display of games by Brownies and a demonstration of various aspects of Tenderfoot, 2nd Class and 1st Class work. There was a model camp, exhibitions and a 'march of badges'. The day ended with a pageant of the Empire and a campfire.

The rally was organised by the following committee:- Miss Drewe (organiser), Miss Pemberton (County Secretary). Miss Staveley (City Commissioner), Miss Allen (County Camp Adviser), Miss Ruck Keene, Mrs Spencer, the Hon. Mrs Mitford, Miss Wells, Mrs Ryman Hall, Miss Hobson and Miss Brownrigg.

According to North Oxford District minutes, it was decided, in 1936, to charge 1d for each badge entry [less than half 1p]. In the same book, in 1937, it is recorded that over 500 presents had been collected for the Stocking Trail and in the same year it was stated that a decision had been made to include Brownies in the Coronation Rally at Wembley in June [George VI]. The Mayor's open-air Coronation Service was held on 9th May, North Oxford District met in Pusey Street. Still in 1937 it was decided to give the Chiefs a piece of silver and a cheque for their Silver Wedding in October. Guides were to give up to 6d and Brownies 1d [12d = 5p].

From North Oxford District's Log:

Miss Caradine has a cine-camera and projector for sub-standard HQ films and is willing to show films.

No comment!

The same Log goes on:

The Commissioner .... HQ were worried about the drop in number of Guides. ... some things were beyond our control -

children grow up sooner, there are more activities for them in their schools, some of the ideas of Guiding have been copied. we might advertise ourselves more - what we stand for and what we do. ... our own personal appearance was of the greatest importance ...

This was written in **1937**.

Also - white socks may not be worn for public occasions, Guide stockings cost 1/11½ at Webbers [2/- = 10p].

In 1937 a Guide from 1st Henley and a Guide from 1st Iffley were chosen by ballot as Oxfordshire representatives to go to London to see the Coronation of King George VI. Perhaps each Division had a place? Church Parades were held to celebrate the Coronation. References appear in the City minutes to a Coronation Camp to which one Ranger or Guide would attend from the Division. King George VI was crowned in May, 1937. Elsewhere, in a non-Guide autobiography I have read of a World Camp at Foxlease in 1937, this book referred to rows and rows of Army tents.

In 1938 visits abroad were still taking place, Rangers from South Division went to Our Chalet where they met Lady B-P. The following is from an account by a lady who was in 5th North Oxford Girl Guide Company, from 1938-1943. It is a typical account of Guiding at that time and makes one wonder how the girls had time for anything other than Guides! I must say that I remember Miss Alden as a kind and caring lady.

Captain was Miss Kathleen Alden and later Mrs Joyce Tory. Meetings were held in the garden of The Croft, Wolvercote or Cutteslowe Hall. Church Parades were at St Michael & All Angels in Lonsdale Road, Division Parades were in Christchurch Cathedral. Summer camps were at High Lodge, Blenheim Palace and day camps at Beanwood.

My first Guide Meeting was at The Croft. [Miss Alden's home].
I learnt how to cut turf, lay and light a fire and cook on it -

cheese dreams and dampers, Afterwards all traces of a fire had to be removed, the turf replaced and watered.

Miss Alden was very strict, she could reduce us to jelly, hence her nick-name - Jelly. Uniform had to be immaculate, ties (triangular) neatly folded and pressed, badges, belt and shoes absolutely gleaming. Patrol points were awarded for same. Every meeting began with Inspection and Patrol Drill. In our pockets we had to have 2 pennies (for the 'phone), a clean hanky, paper and pencil and a safety pin.

Each patrol had a large wooden box with a lid and padlock, usually made by a father, painted by the Guides. Mine was Holly red. The box held useful things; rope, pencils, paper, bandages, slings, dry kindling, compass, scissors, knife, map, etc. A Patrol Flag was attached to a Patrol stick. I well remember embroidering Holly on a piece of old sheet then hemming it. Flags and boxes marked out Patrol Corners.

We were taught signalling, Morse and Semaphore over distances, First Aid, mapping - in the war signposts had been removed. We either cycled or walked everywhere. Knotting was a great feature and games which trained our powers of observation and memory. We did a great deal of tracking, laying the trail with sticks and stones.

We made collections of leaves and flowers, we could recognise every type of tree and wild flower. Bird watching walks were on most Sunday afternoons around the Water Eaton Manor area, we learnt to identify common birds.

Starry nights saw us outside the Hall being taught to identify the main constellations. We often ended meetings with a camp fire sing-song, we had a 'log fire' with red crepe paper and an electric light bulb and we sang by the light of the fire. Many songs were in three or four parts and it did sound nice. We sang Taps at the end.

On Saturday morning we collected the waste paper from the Super Cinema and carried it to a depot in St Aldates. We knitted socks, gloves and balaclava helmets for the Forces. On or near Thinking Day we would have a special ceremony and camp fire. Lighting a candle for each country where there were Guides, many suffering because of the war, they were specially remembered in Prayers.

When we went to camp all the equipment and all the Guides piled into an open-top lorry and were driven from the Hall to the site, returning the same way. We would pitch the bell tents, dig latrines and put up canvas screens, dig a grease-pit, cut turf for the cooking fire and put up a mackintosh roof. An enormous number of wooden gadgets were made from wood which we cut and lashed together (an art learnt at meetings). We made tables, shoe racks, clothes hooks for the tent pole, stands for pots - you name it, we made it.

Our beds were groundsheets on the grass, two blankets fastened with blanket pins and a sheet lining. Pillows were our kitbags. Everything had to be off the ground to keep dry. We took turns as the wood, water, mess or cook patrol.

During the Winter we hemmed squares of butter muslin in assorted sizes, sewing on china beads at intervals. These were to cover food in camp, jugs of milk and so on. Food was cooked in huge dixies which quickly became blackened by smoke. Before striking camp these had to be cleaned to their original gleaming state, very hard work with a little hot water, some wood ash and wire wool. Our fingers were often raw by the time we had finished. Each night at the end of campfire, the cook patrol produced steaming mugs of hot cocoa. Breakfast was always porridge. On wet mornings the cooks had to be up extra early to light the fire and get the porridge ready on time. We always had a 'rest hour' from 2-3 pm, when we had to be quiet and stay in one place.

One afternoon was visitors' Day. The local people, the Vicar and any parents were welcome to come and look at the campsite and were given tea which meant extra work for the cooks who were expected to produce fairly thin b&b, jam, cake and tea. [Pre-sliced bread did not exist before the War.] *Sometimes the Vicar would take a service in camp but we usually attended the parish Church on Sunday morning or evening. Local shops delivered all food which had been ordered some weeks before camp began.*

North Oxford minutes record that instead of the usual Spring training at Eynsham in 1939, Oxfordshire would be going to Foxlease at a cost of approximately 10/- [50p].   The first of many County trainings at Foxlease.

A quote from the City Minutes for 24th November 1938:

1st Class Brownie Exam.

A request had been received from Miss Chapman, examiner for East and West Oxford Districts, that the date of this test be fixed in a similar manner to the Guide Tests. It was agreed the Test should take place:-

a) Late March   b) Early July   c) Late November

Times do change!

In 1939, in the City, there was an official unit of Old Guides in existence - forerunner of the Trefoil Guild.

In January 1939 North Oxford's Christmas party was cancelled due to an epidemic of infantile paralysis. This is polio and was a much dreaded illness. Survivors often lived out their lives in an iron lung. My mother was terrified of it and forbad us to swim if there was a single case reported.

An elderly lady told me how Father Christmas always came to the Brownie and Guide Christmas parties at Shotover House. He came down the chimney and stepped out of the fireplace with a sack of wrapped presents for the girls.

Joyce was a Brownie and Guide in Wheatley, under the leadership of Miss Annie Goatley, a very energetic lady who seems to have run the units of Guides and Brownies in Wheatley and Garsington almost single-handed. Mrs Miller, of Shotover House, was at one time District Commissioner and later Division Commissioner. The evening commenced with the excitement of the Brownies, and another night the Guides, being picked up in a chauffeur-driven limousine and whisked off to the party. For most it was their only car ride in the year. The hall of the house would be filled with long tables of wonderful food, the village girls were awed by both variety and quantity. Games would be played and then, the high spot of the party, Father Christmas came down the chimney, stepped out of the fireplace and General and Mrs Miller watched as he distributed presents from his sack.

Joyce told me that it was several years before she realised that a son of the house, John, now Sir John, was Father Christmas. The hearth was large and he could stand comfortably within it, ready to appear at the right moment.

She admitted that, for her, the real highlight of the parties was the ride in the car, hanging on to the strap and feeling thrilled and frightened by the speed.

* * * * * * * * * * * * * * *

I did not like polishing Captain's leather gauntlets when we were orderly patrol. It took a lot of washing to get rid of the smell on our hands. Woe betide us if Captain got shoe polish on her arms.

We lost a point for our patrol at inspection if our knickers were anything other than navy or black.

We wore ETBs. Elastic top and bottom. They were navy blue, a thick worsted material. We wore vests and liberty bodices. These were cotton, tight garments with four tapes, two back and two front, with a suspender attached.

Right: *Miss Rosalie Brown, showing off her new Tawny Owl uniform [Assistant Brownie Guider].*

Below: *1st East Oxford, 1920.*

The Stocking Trail

A nation-wide Stocking Trail was started in 1933 and continued for many years, references to it have surfaced all around the County. The idea was that Companies and Packs made stockings and filled them with sweets and small toys and whole areas would devise original ways of collecting the stockings. For example, one year in Oxford a Trail was conducted across Shotover as a treasure trail. Nationally the stockings could be for any deprived children, for instance, a Jewish school is mentioned, but Oxfordshire's stockings went to Risca which was, and is, a Welsh village.

References to the Stocking Trail in Oxfordshire begin 1934, in 1935 1st East Oxford spent 2s 7d [nearly 13p] on hessian for the stockings, in 1937 they spent tenpence farthing [less than 5p] on hessian and 9d [less than 4p] on wool from Butlers in Cowley Road. In 1938 the hessian was 7d [less than 3p] and the wool and needles 5d [about 2p], from Wyatt & Sons on Carfax. In December 1938 *'Each patrol made and filled a Xmas stocking for Risca.'*

In 1934 the County Minutes reported that in December 1933 700 stockings and about 100 toys and books were collected for the Oxford House Settlement in Risca in time for Christmas. The County minutes:

... many grateful letters saying how much the gifts had been appreciated by the children of unemployed men ...

We have to remember that there had been war, a disastrous General Strike and that Risca was a coal mining area. A Trail was held in 1934 but no results are mentioned. For the 1935 Trail the warden of the Settlement asked for the stockings to be divided into age groups 3-7; 7-12; 12-14 and to be marked for boy or girl. The stockings had to be made of hessian or casement cloth and not exceed 24 inches in length

[~60cms]. The total that year was 400 stockings, 70 extra books and toys and 20 articles of clothing.

In 1937 the North Oxford District Log Book notes that over 500 parcels and stockings were received on the Stocking Trail. The City Coronation Parade in 1937, in the Cathedral, raised a collection of £4 13 11, the expenses were £2, the balance of £2 13 11 was sent to Risca [£2.70p].

The 1938 minutes report that Risca would be asked if they wanted stockings and individual companies would decide if they wished to do their Christmas Good Turn in this way. In 1939 a hand-written letter was received by the County from the secretary of the RISCA UNEMPLOYED CLUB:

On behalf of the committee of the above, I would be grateful if we could enlist your sympathy, once again this Christmas on behalf of the children of our members.

Last Christmas, as on previous occasions, we, through your co-operation, were able to bring joy & gladness to the hearts of a number of boys & girls who would otherwise have lost faith in Santa Claus.

The kindness of the Girl Guides of Oxford in conducting the Stocking Trail & collecting toys for the children of Risca is a very encouraging example of friendship outside our district.

We feel sure that the girls would be amply repaid, could they but see & witness the happiness they had been able to create.

There are a large number of boys & girls who eagerly look forward to the Christmas treat we hope to be able to provide. We trust you may be able to help us, so that they will not be disapointed (sic)

I remain
Yours sincerely

An Idea of the Finances

We have an interesting set of accounts from 1st East Oxford Guides (St Mary & St John), here are some items from the thirties and forties. The Company is open and active now.

1930	Palava (concert)	3s 9d	[about 19p]
1930	1st East, year's post	1/-	[5p)
1931	1st East, year's post	1s 11d	[nearly 10p]
1932	Hire of 'bus for Hampton Poyle	£1	
1933	Registration Certificate	8d	[about 3p]
1934	Annual tip for caretaker	1/-	[5p]
	buns	2/-	[10p]
1935	'Bus to the Follies	10/-	[50p]
	A uniform from funds	9s 5d	[about 47p]
	Oranges	1s 6d	[nearly 8p)
1937	Cakes and refreshments for Christmas Party	12s 1d	[about 60p]
	One year's rent of hall	£1	
1938	Webber's for camp hats	8s 9d	[nearly 44p]
1939	Hire of room for 1938	£1 10s	[£1.50]
	Stamps for 1939	2s	[40p]
1941	Guide Uniform	19s	[95p]
1944	Post for year	6s	[30p]

[Webber's was a big store on the Carfax end of High Street, North side, next to a Sainsbury's.]

Above: *5th East Oxford Guides collecting salvage, 1942/3.*

Right: *Miss Logan's camp licence, duly endorsed, 1942.*

MISS LOGAN

is a qualified camper

Date 13/6/42

Emilon Mann
Guider's Commissioner

Peggy Jackson.
Guider's C.C.A. (on recommendation
C.A.C. England, of Test Examiner)

C.E. Brown.

Endorsed on recommendation
of visiting C.A.

Date Oct. 24th 1942

The War Effort

In the late 1930s the world changed for everyone - including Guides. As early as September 1938 the City minutes records that their offer of help to the City ARP officer had been accepted. (Air Raid Precautions).

North Oxford District minutes record in October :

As Guiders were being called up for National Service companies were under-staffed, ... *the Commissioner urged everyone to carry on as best they could as long as possible using PLs when Guiders were not available.* PLs were older then, up to seventeen.

In the same month - *it is not advisable for Guides to be out after 8 pm and Brownies not after dark.* Uniform to be worn only when on National Service. There was the vexed question of what to do with evacuees. Some Guiders offered to have evacuated Guides in their companies.

Guides helped the war effort in many ways, some seem fantastic now but at the time were vital to the war effort Many units saved jam jars, newspapers and waste paper. In this way the Guides earned funds for themselves and/or for such organisations as the Red Cross or the BP fund, at the same time they helped the salvage effort. The work of salvage went on for years after the war, remember, there was still some rationing when Queen Elizabeth was crowned in 1953.

Guides collected rose hips for vitamin rich rose hip syrup, some went over the hills and downs collecting wild flowers and herbs for doctors; many companies demonstrated camp cooking on the streets in case of blitz bombing; most learnt and taught first aid; most units organised salvage efforts. In May 1939 Guides in Oxford were helping as messengers with the evacuation of London school children. Guide meetings were suspended by Government order for one month.

Throughout the war Guides helped the Dig for Victory campaign by cultivating spare land at their meeting places, schools and Churches. They grew vegetables - in particular cabbages. Many Guides became inspired to take the Emergency Helper badge in order to be ready to help in the case of enemy action. In 1939, within the County, a loss of Guiders to National Service was reported, some Guiders were coming into the County with evacuee children. New companies were being formed and existing ones enlarged to cope with the evacuated girls. Suggestions were made about improvising uniforms because of clothes'-rationing.

An offer was made to the WVS [now the WRVS] to include teachers and helpers in Guiders' Training Camps. A maximum 25% of non Guide evacuee children were permitted at company camps. There was a great deal of concern in the early days of the war about the possibility of gas attacks. Memories of the Great War were fresh. North Berkshire Rangers, now in Oxfordshire, joined the ARP and were formed into a Decontamination Squad, in case of gas.

The Guide Lats were confiscated by the ARP, we had to be ready to put them up in two minutes if there was a gas attack. At the practice sessions, each Ranger put on a huge overall, rubber gloves, wellingtons, gas mask and she took up her position inside her lat cubicle armed with a bucket of whitewash and a massive decorating brush. As each mock casualty arrived the Rangers had to instruct him (they were all men) to strip off his clothing, which was bagged up and would have been burnt in a real attack, then cover the casualty from head to foot with whitewash. One Ranger was horrified to find her first 'casualty' was the local Curate. We did not know with what we would paint real casualties but it would not have been whitewash.

The Ranger who whitewashed the curate reports:

He kept his underpants on but I was scarlet with embarrassment. Goodness knows how I would have coped had we done it in earnest on naked bodies.

It is also reported that these North Berkshire Rangers made daily newspaper collections and collected bones from pubs and cafes, etc. As they collected they sang:

It's quite well known, a cutlet bone will make an aeroplane.

<u>1939 in Kennington</u>.

I was 13 and looking forward to my first Guide camp, to be held in Lyndhurst, in the New Forest. Our Captain was excited too, she called to see my mother the day before to finalise arrangements, she said she had cooked a ham for our first meal. The following day she called again, almost in tears, she had received a telegram advising us not to go because of the crisis and the possibility of war. We had a day in Bagley Wood and took our picnic food prepared for our journey to camp. Next day we set up camp in the village (Kennington), it was a come-down but no one minded as it was still our first experience and exciting. We learned afterwards that Guides who had gone to camp had been sent home after two days. We had a great week and near the end several of us went to Abingdon to help with the evacuee children from London. We delivered notes to the families who were to care for the children. On the Sunday morning, 3rd September, my PL and I cycled to Abingdon and helped until afternoon. When we arrived back at camp there was an empty space, war had been declared and Captain, who had lived through the first war and had lost a brother, had struck camp straight away as she did not know what might happen. I did not camp again until after the war but I will never forget sleeping on a palliasse filled with straw and using trench lats!

In January 1939 the North Oxford District minute book says:

The Commissioner then stated what Guiders had been asked to do towards Air Raid Defence: i.e.

*a)   help evacuate London school children, which would
mean taking care of the children arriving in Oxford, waiting to
be taken to the country,*

*b)   supply volunteers for report centres which would
require a staff of 15, to be in action only during an actual Air
Raid. Classes would be held from Wed Oct 5th at 8 pm in
Alma Hall preferably for Rangers and Guiders with office
experience who would volunteer for this work.*

*Those willing to help in evacuating children were to apply to Miss
Johnstone ... giving home address, business address, telephone
number, times when free, mode of transport by which arriving.*

*It was suggested that Guides could make various direction
signs for such an emergency.*

These requests gaily mention telephone numbers, not many had
telephones in 1939. The entry goes straight into a request for jumble!
During the war the Guide magazine exhorted the girls to
further efforts and at times offered advice on make-do-and-
mend and on matters of economy - both patriotic activities.

Economy in coal - *one pound of washing soda dissolved in a
large pail of water and sprinkled over the coal will make it
burn longer and brighter.* Coal was rationed.

Emergency boot polish - *where there is no boot polish in the
house lemon juice makes an excellent substitute: rub a few
drops briskly on black or brown leather boots and they will
have a brilliant polish.* Lemons were unobtainable in the war!

To clean a mackintosh - *a mackintosh that has become hard
may be cleaned thus:- dissolve a handful of best grey lime in
half a pail of water and apply to the stiff parts with a small
sponge.* Mackintoshes, before synthetics and plastics, were
made of a rubberised canvas like material.

Boiled milk - *skin may be prevented from forming on boiled
milk if, as soon as it is boiled, the vessel containing the milk
is placed in cold water until the milk is cold. No skin forms at*

all. In the days before refrigerators any milk left at the end of the day had to be 'scalded', that is, brought to the boil, in order to prevent it going off overnight. It tasted a bit queer on the porridge, I remember.

There are more tips, many concerned with darning socks and stockings and mending clothes. It was a different world.

A report in the Kidlington Village newsletter at the time of the Golden Jubilee of 1st Kidlington Guides gives an account of the war years, patriotism being clearly illustrated in the choice of names for the patrols.

1st Kidlington Guide Company was started in September, 1939 and registered at HQ in the October. The first Captain was Miss Dorothy Bubbers, an evacuee teacher billeted at Thornbury House with a party of girls from East Ham Grammar School. The Company met at St Thomas More Hall with Miss Rose Deeley and Miss Sylvia Thurston as lieutenants. In December 1939 Miss Rose Deeley started the 1st Kidlington Brownie Pack.

Guiding activities were related to the war effort, the patrols were the Searchlight, Victory, Spitfire and Primrose Patrols. In common with most other Guides the girls learnt first aid, morse and semaphore, played tracking and stalking games, conducted salvage operations. They combed the village pushing perambulators and trek carts collecting newspapers, jam jars and rags. They collected books for the forces and in doing this climbed 'the ranks' according to the number of books collected. Most remained Privates but a few became Field Marshals - a great many books were needed to achieve this!

In 1940 and 1941 day camps were held at Gosford Hill Farm, Christmas 1941 saw the first Good Turn Party, the Guides handed over toys they had bought and made to the Radcliffe Infirmary and the Wingfield Hospital, now the Nuffield Orthopaedic Centre. In late 1941 Miss Thurston joined the Women's Land Army and the Summer of 1942 saw a week long camp at Eynsham Park, 16

Guides from Kidlington and 9 from Coombe attended. In 1942 the Good Turn Party produced 300 toys for hospitals. Another Good Turn was helping at Kidlington PO so that Christmas mail would be on time. Some Guides were so dedicated they were working on Christmas Day delivering telegrams. When Miss Bubbers had to return to London, Miss Deeley became Captain and continued to lead the Company until 1953.

In 1943 the Guides camped at Beanwood and in November of that year were part of the 1,500 Guides to greet the Chief Guide in Oxford. In 1944 there was a PL training at Beanwood and a district camp of 40 Guides from Kidlington, Bletchingdon and Islip, the company came second in the county camp competition and attended a parade to St Mary's Church where Lady Goodenough and the Duchess of Marlborough took the salute. During this year the Guides raised funds for the Guide International Service and by Christmas they had raised enough to send a member of the GIS to Warsaw. Not bad for a 5-year-old Company. The Guides celebrated the end of the war with fireworks and a camp at Broughton castle, near Banbury.

In 1999 the unit is still in existence and flourishing.

High School Company, 1934.

72

Public Meeting

Town Hall,

Henley-on-Thames

Saturday, 29th March, 1947

at 3.15 p.m.

Speaker :

The Lady Baden-Powell, G.B.E.

The World Chief Guide

Chairman :

His Worship the Mayor

Come and Bring your Friends

Left: *Henley's big day.*

Below: *From the Brownie Magazine.*

FOLDING UNDERWEAR.

FOLD IN HALF

FOLD IN HALF TWICE

PUT TOES TOGETHER

MAKE BALL

PULL WELT OVER.

Patrol Leader c1949.

War and Peace

The war effort continued in earnest, salvage collections featured very high on the list. It cannot be emphasised too strongly how important this work was, paper was in very short supply, if a housewife wished her purchases of food to be put in a paper bag then she took a bag or two with her, otherwise everything would be tipped into her shopping bag, muddy potatoes and all - no shop carrier bags. Books were in short supply because of the paper shortage, as a child in the war I had no books of my own, only those inherited from my brother. Food was short and imported food almost unobtainable, I did not know what ice cream was, I was too young to remember before the war. I remember after the war I cried when my mother peeled the single banana she had obtained from somewhere to share between my two brothers and I - she took off all the yellow and the inside was white. Every picture I had seen of a banana showed them as yellow! At one time bread was rationed, at another potatoes. Front gardens were dug up and planted with vegetables, stately home owners dug up their lawns and flower beds for the same purpose. Coal was rationed. For a weekend camp we had to take at least one day's ration of meat, either stewing beef or a tin of meat. It all went into a lovely stew. A ration book of stewing beef cost 1/- [5p] and was more or less a handful. For longer camps we took ration cards.

Clothing was rationed by a points system, many things were unobtainable and brand names gave way to the 'Utility' brand. Utility was a standard laid down by the Government for many things, a standard with a minimum quality but also an upper quality to encourage fairness. I still have a book case/cabinet marked Utility and two Utility blankets went to Oxfam recently. Because of the urgent need for metal, garden railings were melted down, saucepans were unobtainable. If saucepan developed a hole (it was before the days of aluminium and pyrex) it was mended with a kit.

The war was an ever present thing, the telegram boy on his red motor bike was dreaded, Mr Churchill's speeches on the wireless were listened to in silence, newspapers were full of horrendous pictures of bomb damage and dog fights (fighter 'plane battles). Gas masks were carried everywhere and lights showing at night were strictly forbidden. When I joined the Guides in November 1947 the Guide Law in my patrol box still carried the eleventh Guide Law - A Guide always carries her gas mask. Dad's Army really happened, my father was in the Home Guard and the ARP. We were still rationed in Coronation year, 1953, but not as severely.

These personal reminiscences may help to put the war into perspective.

By May 1939 Guides in Oxford were already helping with the national war effort. Throughout the war Guides helped the Dig for Victory campaign by cultivating spare land at their meeting places, schools and Churches. They grew vegetables - in particular cabbages. Many Guides were inspired to take the Emergency Helper and other First Aid badges in case of enemy action.

In 1939 a loss of Guiders to the Forces was reported, some Guiders were coming into the County with evacuee children. New companies were being formed and existing ones enlarged to cope with evacuated girls. Suggestions were made about improvising uniforms because of clothes rationing. North Oxford reported an appeal for uniforms for evacuees. Evacuee Guiders were given temporary warrants. As said earlier, an offer was made to the WVS (now the WRVS) to include teachers and helpers in Guiders' Training

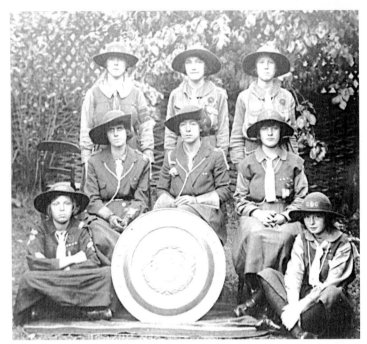

3rd Headington Guides won the Oxford Folk Music Society Dance Competition 1922.

Wantage Market Square full of Guides - unknown occasion.

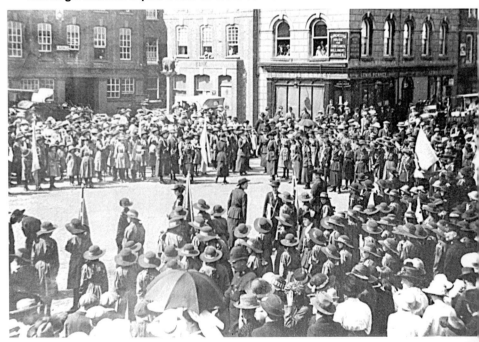

Camps and a maximum of 25% of non Guide evacuee children were permitted at company camps.

In 1940 the Annual Church Parade of the City Division was cancelled because Christchurch Cathedral had insufficient bomb shelters. Some Summer camps were cancelled in that year because of food rationing and transport difficulties - petrol was strictly rationed. Gift days for foreign wounded soldiers were held and in East Oxford PLs took gifts of food to the wounded soldiers in the Cowley Road Hospital. One unit in the District raised 36/- [£1.80] for the Air Ambulance Fund.

Many patrols organised themselves into areas and prepared themselves to go out and help in the event of a raid. Hikes were organised to collect acorns and horse chestnuts for the war effort, many units and patrols collected rose hips for rose hip syrup. In 1940 several units in North Oxford were preparing to go on a fruit and hop picking camp in Kent.

In April 1941 the eighth Annual Meeting of the East Oxford District L.A. reported that -

... although war jobs had been hard to find. Allotments at Iffley and Marston were being worked and the proceeds of the sale of vegetables ... to the Red Cross. ... 20th November, 1940 our Headquarters was requisitioned by the Army [Alma Hall] *and but for the kind hospitality of the Wesley Hall folk we should have been without a roof to shelter us.* [Jeune Street Methodist Church Hall].

On 12th March 1942 the minutes reported that:

Our District HQ was once more in our possession and most of the damage had been made good.

The County Commissioner, Lady Evelyn Mason, resigned in 1941 because the York Conference had suggested that younger Commissioners were desirable. Her resignation was not accepted because all the young Guiders were on active service. She resigned successfully in 1942.

Empire Week was an annual occurrence and an opportunity to give to a fund for the war effort. In 1941, it was suggested that this week should be an opportunity to give half a day's income or one day's pocket money to the Air Ambulance or Lifeboat Funds.

Some things carried on regardless of the war, City Division were involved in correspondence with the Town Hall about a Division badge. This was to be the 'cow-in-a-puddle' emblem of Oxford City. This later became our Guide County Badge. Also in this year Headington Guides gave a demonstration of emergency cooking. In the Picture Post a photograph appeared showing Guides from Oxfordshire collecting wild flowers and nettles for a local doctor. A War Service Badge was introduced for 96 hours of war work. Patrols in East Oxford raised money to buy wool to knit socks for evacuees. In Thinking Day ceremonies Guides in occupied countries were remembered specially.

In August 1941 2nd Witney Guides held a Summer camp at Eynsham Hall, home of Lady Evelyn Mason, County Commissioner. An extract from the camp log reads:

They had an extra long time to chatter in bed before we sang 'Taps' from the tents. It sounded very nice in the still of the evening to the Guiders standing outside and made us realise more than ever how near God is to us all. That night an alert sounded and I dressed partly and put on my coat and rested on the bed just in case the girls had to be called but the camp slept on peacefully and I do not think anyone knew the siren had sounded. Fortunately it did not last long and I heaved a sigh of relief when I heard the All Clear about half an hour later.

It is a tremendous responsibility to take Guides to camp any time but in war time it must have been awesome.

I remember that in the 1940s a Guide could camp for a week for 12/6d [less than 63p].

In the midst of war Guides and Scouts mourned the death of Lord Baden-Powell, he died at his home, Pax Tu, in Kenya. A memorial service was hurriedly arranged in the Cathedral in January 1941.

1930
The caption reads
OXFORD'S DISTINGUISHED VISITORS:
Left to Right, in front - Lord Baden-Powell (Chief Scout), the Mayor of Oxford and Lady Baden-Powell (Chief Guide). Back Row, left to right - Brig-Gen A D Miller, Sir Montgu Burrows, the Mayoress of Oxford, Lady Burrows and Sir Michael Sadler.

A 935

GIRL GUIDES

B.-P. MEMORIAL FUND

(Opening Date April 23rd, 1942)

1st Fritwell Coy.

THANK YOU FOR YOUR GIFT OF

£ : 15 s. d.

which has been lent to the Government by investment in National Savings Funds until it can be spent on a Memorial to our Founder.

Louisa Atkinson.

Chief Commissioner

(See over)

1st Fritwell Guides' B-P Memorial Fund receipt and voucher, 1942. The money (15/- or 75p) was invested in National Savings until after the War and then paid into the Memorial Fund.

BP HQ 1942

NOT TRANSFERABLE

B-P Memorial Fund

GIRL GUIDES

1st Fritwell Coy.

COMPANY OR PACKS REGISTERED TITLE

PURCHASE PRICE

15/-

Give-Lend Voucher

1

NATIONAL SAVINGS UNIT

I hereby declare that the GIFT indicated on this Voucher has been LENT to the Government by investment in National Savings funds until such time as it shall be deemed suitable for it to be spent on a Memorial to our Founder

Louisa Atkinson.

Chief Commissioner

20 MAY 1942

DATE OF ISSUE

One company of Guides ran an allotment, another knitted for the Navy. Arrangements were made for Guides and Rangers to get cooking fires going and hot meals ready after a blitz, all cooking to be done in double saucepans. It must be remembered that other towns and cities were blitzed, Oxford expected the same. There was also the real possibility of an invasion and preparations were in hand for such a disaster.

In 1942 an Oxford University District was formed under the leadership of Miss McNamara. It was disbanded in 1954.

A HQ directive in early 1942, read out to every Division and District meeting in the County states:

Pacifists in the Guide Movement

A girl, on becoming a member of the Girl Guide Movement, promises to do her duty to God and the King. It is obvious that her conception of what her duty to her Country is, must be subject to and governed by her conception of her duty to God. So long as her view of her duty to God allows her to remain loyal to the laws of her Country, for her loyalty to her Country implies loyalty to its laws - she can continue to subscribe to the Guide Movement and remain a Member; but when her views on her duty to God are such as to bring her in conflict with the laws of her Country, then there can be no alternative but for her to resign from the Movement.

The Guide and Scout Movements recognise that certain of their Members conscientiously object to taking life, as for example those who belong to the Society of Friends, but they are prepared to help their Country in other ways, such as ambulance work.

Where a Guide's conscientious opinions make it impossible for her to help her country in war time in any form of National Service such as first aid, and various forms of Civil Defence, it is clear that she cannot keep her first promise or the second one to help other people at all times.

QUARTERMASTER CERTIFICATE

M⁓ BEAL

HAS QUALIFIED AS A CAMP QUARTERMASTER

Catharine T. Bowen - EXAMINER
            CAMP ADVISER

DATE October 1ˢᵗ 1946.

Mrs Beal's Camp QM Certificate signed by Miss Bowen, 1946.

The Guide International Service Badge, 1942-52.

A Guide enrolled in 1st Grimsbury Guides in 1942, remembers that they met in the Old Blue Bird Hotel in a small back room. *I can vividly remember going with my patrol leader, (a London evacuee) to feed pigeons used by the Home Guard to carry messages. We collected jam jars from everyone in our street, our company was paid by the hundred jars. When the Autumn came we could be found all along Salt Lane or the Broughton Road to the Giants' Caves picking rose hips which brought in revenue for the Company and were made in vitamin rich Rose Hip Syrup.*

I was a Brownie and a Guide in Kidlington during the war. We were involved with Miss Deeley in war efforts continually. We collected newspapers in the High Street on Saturdays and later we had the book drive to find reading matter for the lads in the forces. Each Guide could win a Sergeant badge by collecting so many books. If we collected a certain number (in the hundreds) we could become Field Marshals! Some of us did! I remember having Socials to make money to send a Guider worker [GIS] into Europe after the war and thinking how brave these women were to go when it was all such a mess out there.

We camped every year. My first camp was in Eynsham Park. We could not show lights after dark because enemy 'planes might see us. It was 1942 I think. I remember Church Parades and village Parades when we marched round the village of Kidlington. A particular hazard was having the heel of your shoe stepped on by the Guide directly behind you and then having to keep hopping in time with the march until the shoe was back on again. Marching practice was a regular part of Guide meetings. Outdoor cooking and campfires were my favourite occupations then and still are today.

A follow up to the reference to pigeons in Grimsbury, pigeons were used for messages in order to maintain radio silence and thus avoid the enemy's intelligence system, The Grimsbury Rangers had entire charge of the pigeon loft and sent and received messages as their War Effort. On Thinking Day, 1943, a carrier pigeon was sent from Banbury by the 1st Grimsbury Rangers to the Chief Guide. The message read: *Oxfordshire sends greetings to Guides, throughout the World, and looks forward to the time when we shall all be united in the cause of peace.*

In 1942 the County re-organised itself into five Divisions.

There was a Housewives' Scheme planned in 1942, carried out in '43, by the WVS. Emergency cooking demonstrations were to be held in each District. There were to be two demonstrations by Miss Axtell's Company in East Oxford; one by Miss McDonald's in the South and one by Miss Bowen's in Headington. In 1943 it was reported that 5th East Oxford (Miss Axtell's) gave a demonstration of 'Blitz' cooking to the WVS in Cowley. This work was *'greatly admired'.*

In 1942, war or not, camping went ahead. It was reported that there were 14 camps at The Follies at Wytham with about 28 Guiders, 9 Rangers, 8 Sea Rangers and 150 Guides. On 28th September 1942 City Division collected 140lbs of Rose Hips, which earned them 19/- [20/- = £1]. The Division made this up to 30/- [£1.50] and sent it to the B-P memorial fund.

Census figures for the County: 1941, 3,867; 1943, 3,876. This was despite the return home of many evacuee children . In the City the figures were: Total, 1,420 girls and 79 adults. There were; 532 Brownies; 781 Guides; 22 Sea Rangers; 29 Rangers; 3 Extension Packs and 1 Company.

The Chief Guide visited Oxford in November 1943. There was a meeting for LAs and interested public at Rhodes House on the 4th, there would be a Guide Guard of Honour. On the 5th there was a march past in Tom Quad, Christchurch followed by a meeting in the Town Hall.

From the Banbury area:

My best memory was in 1943 when Lady Baden-Powell visited us in Banbury Town Hall. I was too young to know where all the Guides came from but the big room upstairs was packed and we sang a nonsense song to her 'As I was going to Banbury'. I met her again at the Sheldonian Theatre some time later. She addressed us indoors and then inspected us outside. She was just going past me when she noticed I had my Little House Emblem. She came back and congratulated me and said 'well done, little Guide'. I expect she thought I was younger than I was (I haven't grown much bigger now).

On Saturday, May 22nd 1943 Guides in Abingdon sacrificed their monthly hike to march in the 'Wings for Victory' Parade. It poured with rain but the Guides marched well, they had practised under the guidance of the Home Guard. In November 1943 a County Rally was visited by Lady Baden-Powell and 219 Guides and Brownies travelled by train to the Rally. Some of the girls had not been on a train before.

In 1943 5th East Oxford Guides bought a trek cart for £22. The money had been raised by the collection and sale of jam jars and newspapers - part of their war effort but with the bonus of being a fund-raising exercise. In the same year three PLs from the same company became the first in the County to qualify for a Patrol Leader's Camp Permit. North Oxford District also bought a trek cart, for £20, they intended charging for its use.

The Guides received an invitation to a Scout Service to be held in the Sheldonian Theatre on 22nd April 1944 and 500 Guides attended. The next minutes refer to the Scout Service as being on 20th February, a much more likely date.

During 1944 War Service Guide Clubs were formed. A West Indian Contingent at an ATS camp near Bicester asked to be put in touch with local Companies as they wished to keep a link with Guiding. It was suggested that they form their own club and a copy of the

Oxford Training Programme was sent to them. Permission was given for a Ranger Club in the ATS camp at Deddington.

The County Commissioner circulated a list of Post War Aims for Guiding:

1. *What are the fundamental things and the transitory things of Guiding?*
2. *Definite service to the Community, are war services to be carried into peace time?*
3. *What help do we need from other people and bodies outside our own organisation?*
4. *How are we to convey to the general Public what Guiding really is?*

In 1944 rooms in the Beanwood Cottage were allocated to Divisions to equip and decorate.

A great effort for salvage was a national necessity, newspapers and jam jars were particularly needed and Guides all over the County co-operated in this essential work. The WVS co-ordinated some of the jam jar salvage. This salvage effort went on long after the end of the war, the following quote refers to the late '40s and early '50s

A Guide from 5th East Oxford reports:

I got the shock of my little life - Daddy worked on the Oxford Mail, I thought it a certainty that our patrol would collect the most newspapers. I bounced home from Guides burbling about collecting newspapers and please would Daddy bring me extra newspapers every day?

He refused.

I was stunned!

He explained that it would be wrong to bring me extra newspapers from the office to be sold because the Oxford Mail had to buy recycled newsprint. It would be stealing and immoral as the firm sold the leftover papers itself.

It was my introduction to moral values.

I forgave him.

Miss MacDonald told the story of a very efficient and self confident patrol leader who was to take a trek cart full of jam jars to Cooper's - Frank Cooper's Marmalade Factory in the Botley Road, where MFI is now. Miss MacDonald watched from the shop in New Inn Hall Street, where she worked, her Guides looked very smart as they pulled the loaded trek cart from the Wesley Memorial Hall towards Queen Street. A few minutes later they came back again, the trek cart still loaded. Miss MacDonald slipped out to investigate. The efficient patrol leader was flustered and explained that Cooper's did not want the jam jars. She had taken the trek cart to G R Cooper, the big hardware shop in Queen Street, the present site of the Westgate Centre. Miss MacDonald was hard put not to laugh. She explained, gently, that the jars were to go to Frank Cooper's and the Guides set off again. The efficient patrol leader took a little time to recover from her gaffe.

During the war 1st Grimsbury had outings to St Louis private school. Each Guide took a sausage and the head greeted them with a large frying pan and a huge piece of lard and they cooked their sausages. They camped at Broughton Castle, Lord Saye & Sele was the local Scout Commissioner and loved to visit their campfires.

An unexpected meeting:-

To enable our London colleagues to have a break from war-torn surroundings and nightly bombing, some of us in the Oxford-based Civil Service volunteered to swop with them for two weeks. Thus did two young Civil Service secretaries - also Guide Lieutenants - find themselves steaming up to London.

It has to be appreciated that this 'adventure' really was such for us. (As war-time children we had probably only once set foot in the capital.) This was the height of the V2 rocket bombs; the blackout; the barrage balloons and, for those unfortunate enough to live in London, beds in the tube stations. Much then against our parents' wishes, off we set and found that we were to stay at 'Our Ark'. This was the original Guide home off Buckingham Palace Road and was being used as a hostel for female workers in the City.

It was clear when we arrived that 'something was up'. There was much polishing and the show cases holding the china bearing the 'Our Ark' logo were opened up and the contents carefully washed. Arriving in a few days was the World Chief Guide, Lady Baden-Powell. A special meal was being prepared and, of course, the very special china was to be used. We were bidden to attend! I don't, I am afraid, remember the meal but I do know that very shortly after eating it, the air raid siren sounded against a background of explosions from the rockets and we hastened to basement shelter. Most sat on the floor, Lady Baden-Powell had the armchair and to my horror asked me to sit on one of the arms. I felt that I had no choice! She, of course, regaled us with 'yarns' whilst I sat with ever increasing embarrassment, much too close to this, to me then, somewhat illustrious person. I can only say I would have rather sat on the floor!

There was a footnote to the above:

V2 rockets won't mean much! They followed the so-called 'Doodle-bugs', the V1s, and were worse in that they were noiseless until they dropped and exploded. (The V1s, apparently, were a bit like motor bikes in the sky.)

Nina admits to finding the bombs and being London in war-time very exciting.

One Guide in Oxford had appendicitis but did not tell anyone of her pain. Her headmistress had told the girls that it was unpatriotic to be ill in war time as the hospitals and doctors were needed for the service men.

It was a different world, half-day school because evacuees from London had our school for half the day, so plenty of time to cycle around map-reading, there were no sign posts in the war, a strategy to confuse any invading enemy. Some Guides lost their fathers. We had 'foreign' girls in the Company, from the USA, whose mothers made super cakes from the US PX sources. On the whole, although I shouldn't say so, we were advantaged by being the age we were in the war, slightly older and we would have gone into the forces, as it was we did what the older ones would have done and it was a super training for life.

In the war PLs were responsible for seeing each member of their patrols home before going home themselves. There was no thought of muggings or rape, indeed girls of 16-ish, as PLs were at that time, would not have known the words.

Some of 5th East Oxford War Efforts under the leadership of Miss M W Axtell, not all from the same source:

Yes, we taught the WVS how to build a field oven (don't know how we knew how) and all about hay-box cooking. In the event of invasion we were to report and help with feeding people in the area.

It was wonderful to see the admiration in the eyes of adults at the skill the children demonstrated in this way.

[Emergency cooking]

We collected newspaper and I remember the big hall at Jeune Street being stacked high on all sides.

We collected ... to help finance the war effort, jam jars, newspaper, packaging, foil etc.

We made up parcels to take to the wounded.

We (unwillingly) <u>DUG for VICTORY</u> planting all kinds of vegetables on land in Cowley, Iffley and East Oxford.

We assisted, by being patients, in major Air Raid exercises involving all emergency services. I remember being hoisted to the top of one of the chimneys at Morris Motors to give the fire service practice in getting down a badly injured person! I had (labelled) major internal injuries and two broken legs. This sort of injury was the most popular since it meant a ride in an ambulance. I'd hardly ever been driven in anything except Captain's car - if she had petrol.

Guides were used as messengers by various organisations in the City - some formed themselves into <u>Street Patrols</u> ready to help should an emergency arise.

Camping in the war presented special problems, not least the rationing of food. Guides were not allowed to camp out of the County, Eynsham Hall, the home of Lady Evelyn Mason, one time CC, was a popular site. The USA army had a base in the grounds and would sometimes tease the Guides by demanding to inspect gas masks and identity cards before allowing them through the gate for a day out.

We camped at Nuneham Courtenay, we celebrated VJ Day there with an enormous bonfire.

The Lady Evelyn Mason - a great character.

It is my first recollection of seeing a coloured person.
[US army personnel at Eynsham Hall]

I remember a meeting in a hall in St Giles ... it was to gather together all interested in Guiding as the war was over and we had to find a new CC ... I remember talking to some high-up Guide person there ...

1944 saw the first Christmas Camp held by 5th East Oxford. Patrol Leaders and Seconds, along with the Guiders camped in the cottage at Beanwood over the New Year. They trekked out from Oxford, they cooked out of doors but slept upstairs in the cottage. They were definitely fun camps, which were greatly enjoyed by all who had the privilege to attend. The camps continued for some years.

On New Year's Eve the campers hung stockings on the huge mantelpiece in the big room and everyone put a small gift in each stocking, a very small gift, costing just pence, and suitably wrapped. They played games until midnight when the little window in the

5th East Oxford Guiders at Beanwood, note the thatched cottage.

5th East Oxford Leaders and Seconds off to Christmas Camp at Beanwood, 1950.

upstairs room was opened, if the wind was right then the bells of Oxford ringing in the New Year could be heard clearly .

Next morning, early, Father Christmas and the Christmas Fairy would clump up the stairs in their Wellington boots and distribute the stockings to the campers, still in their sleeping bags. The two would be suitably dressed, Father Christmas in red robes, beard and wellies, the Fairy, usually the biggest of the Guides, wore a flimsy dress, silver wings, a tinsel crown - and wellie boots. She carried a star-topped wand.

The cottage was not the warmest place to spend a Winter weekend but we loved it. It was pretty cold going to the lat shed. The big room had a huge chimney, we could see the sky, it was possible to stretch belief and imagine Father Christmas arriving. We each took a lump of coal, the Scouts collapsed with laughter when they saw us loading coal onto the trek cart. We cooked outside but the coal was a useful addition to wood in the Cottage fireplace.

Bullingdon's first Annual Report, in 1945, records that at a Rally in Oxford 1,500 Guides and Brownies attended and it therefore seems certain that the membership of the Movement in the County must have been in excess of 1,500.

The Guide International Service - 1944-5

After the war there was a refugee problem such as the world had not known before and in 1944, in anticipation of the crisis, the Guide International Service was formed to help with displaced persons. A number of units attended talks by GIS members and this helped them to understand the importance of the GIS work. In 1944 a scheme was devised to raise even more money for the GIS than in 1943. It was felt that something dramatic was needed to keep the girls' interest.

The result was a 'Journey to Europe'. Oxfordshire Guides took part in this scheme, it worked like this:

Companies, Packs and individuals were invited to make an imaginary journey to a capital city in Europe where there had been Guides before the war. As money was raised for the GIS so tickets and passports were 'purchased'. Travel fares had to be paid before the voyage began. It cost 15/- [75p] for a whole company to travel to the British coast, when that was paid the company received a miniature train and an illustrated map of the world on which to follow their progress. A passport was opened for them at the GIS office and at each stage of the journey the card was signed. It cost the company another 15/- for the boat fare to Europe, custom charges were 5/- [25p] and the final ticket to travel in Europe cost £2. Working passages could be negotiated - for instance, a holder of the Knitter's proficiency badge could reduce her fare by half if she knitted an article of clothing for a refugee child.

The Journey scheme proved popular and whole Divisions embarked on journeys and money was raised for the GIS. It is hard to imagine the enormity of the problem in Europe at that time, the GIS did valuable work and its money was raised by and from the Guides of the time, a time when money was short and conditions in this country far from ideal after the devastation of war. The map gave pre-war figures for the numbers of Guides in each country, Great Britain: 525,276; Ireland: 2,884; Luxembourg: 302; Second largest, Poland: 62,857; France: 24,087.

In Bullingdon's Annual Report of 1945: *'dogged determination, much hard work and the refusal to accept defeat'* were given as the reasons for the continuation of Guiding in spite of the national call-up of women under 45. It also says that the most outstanding achievement of the Division has been the raising of money for the GIS, the target set was £50 but in six months £200 was raised and in eighteen months, £376.

The money was obtained almost entirely by the efforts of the children themselves, through Entertainments, Bring and Buy Sales, Jumble Sales, Fun Fairs, Fetes, all of which received the support and co-operation of the members of the Local Association. In some cases it was the result of real self-sacrifice on the part of the Guides and Brownies, who went without such things as Christmas cards, sweets and pocket money, or else worked hard collecting wood, cleaning shoes, weeding or earning money in some other way. Thus every Guide and Brownie helped to raise an average of nearly £1 a head, and in the giving they themselves received untold joy and happiness.

In Oxfordshire Guides raised, for the GIS, £410 11s 4d in 1944 and £963 9s 0d in 1945, a great deal of money at the time. In 1944 GIS workers from the County included: Miss Doreen Mills (Henley), working with the laboratory unit attached to the mobile hospital team; Miss Nora Johnson (Oxford City), worked with the cookery unit, both were commended. These two, along with Miss MacIntosh, (Oxford City) were accepted by the GIS and passed the 'camping test'. Miss Margery Walkinshaw spent three months in a displaced persons' camp in Germany. Other Oxfordshire Guiders served in the GIS.

In the GIS I went out with general team 107 in the beginning of April 1945 to Tilburg in Holland where we worked at any job we could until Holland was liberated. We then went to Rotterdam and worked with the local Red Cross and other organisations on emergency feeding, clothing, health, etc, gradually handing over to the locals. From there we went to Belsen Camp, the team worked with the other teams there, I worked with the babies in the children's hospital. The next move was to Fallinbostal where I ran a feeding scheme for the camp children. In the Winter we moved again to Gebertshagen, near Brunswick. It was an area with many DP camps [Displaced Persons/refugees] our job was to supply what we could in welfare 'extras', clothing and handcraft materials if we had them. We also helped with repatriations and any job which turned up. After some time there I changed to the kitchen/canteen team and on to child feeding in the Rhur. At first we had a large kitchen with German helpers where food was prepared and delivered to the kindergartens in containers, we used to drive our trucks and drop off the full containers and pick up empties.

After some months we took over the organisation of a larger area, two of us on the job of looking after supplies of food and looking over the kitchens. The rest of the team doing general welfare work. I had a 3-ton truck and took delivery of sacks of peas, beans, dried soup, vegetables and almost any sort of food. Sometimes I had to go to the Docks at Duisburg or to Aachen and load up, returning to our central store at Bochum. Bochum was one of the towns which was badly destroyed as it was an engineering area. Gradually, as conditions improved, we were able to hand over to the locals and we then did more youth work, camps for unfit mine apprentices and children's camps at which youth leaders were given camp training.

Reading this account, one has to feel enormous respect for the GIS ladies. They lived in a world where young ladies rarely ventured abroad, they were not used to the appalling conditions in the camps. They were adaptable, brave, resourceful people. It makes our motto 'Be Prepared' come to life. The GIS was a project of which we can be proud.

Bullingdon subscribed £50 to the Baden-Powell Memorial Fund in 1945, a total of £426 had been raised. To put this sum of money into perspective, the accounts for the Division, as recorded in the Annual Report, quoted earlier, show an expenditure of £37 10s 6d for the period 1942-45 with a surplus of £4 6s 7d and the *total* membership of the Division in the 1945 Census was 374 in 29 units.

In 1947 there was a regional camp at Elton, a Rally in Hyde Park and a Royal March Past.

You asked why marching was practised in 1947? I know, because I practised every week, we had to do it properly. Miss Walkinshaw used to be there I remember. I remember marching past the grand platform in the Mall, smartly eyes righting. The Queen (then Princess Elizabeth) and Princess Margaret were so small and wore a lot of make up. I remember we slept in the deep underground shelters. I could hear the underground train above it. We went down in great lifts and the bunks were in narrow tunnels. On the Monday we went to Hyde Park to watch the dancing which was very exciting.

This march past was for the International Folk Dance Festival, one lot of minutes record that the girls *must be drilled* and that sheets of instructions had been received from H.Q. According to the City minutes an ATS instructor was involved in the training of the marchers. A large party of Oxfordshire Guides went to the Rally and March Past, One company sent two carloads.

One Guide from Kidlington went to the camp, associated with the Festival, at Chigwell. Jean kept a log, these are extracts:

I passed my 1st Class in time for my name to go forward, I was very excited over it. The kit list rather bothered me as everything had to be blue but after borrowing and making many things my kit was complete. Losing my kit list a week before the camp made me rely on memory. After doing two exams at school in the morning, I ate a hurried dinner and caught the train and 'bus to Kidlington. My insides felt queer with excitement. I had a huge supper pack and a tin of biscuits and a few odds and ends packed in my ruc-sack while out of the end of a bulging kit-bag stuck three pointed articles looking like weapons but were gadget wood. They were rather dangerous on crowded stations.

I caught the 4 pm train to Oxford, with Mummy, as she stepped out four Guides scrambled into the carriage, kit bags almost flew through the door as the train started to move. We soon got to know each other and very soon I suggested eating - I was always hungry. We were met at Paddington and taken across London to Liverpool Street by underground and put on a train to Ilford and then on another to Grange Hill. We caught a 'bus to Chigwell Row and walked through two or three camps before reaching ours. There was no lights out as Guides were still arriving at 11 pm. We discovered that another Jean and I had identical pyjamas, mine were too tight at the hips which caused hilarity. I was silly to have taken new pyjamas to camp without trying them. We had a practice march on the common on Saturday. My Aunty came to see me before supper and I went to the gate to see my Granny. Next morning we struck camp and went by 'bus into London for the March Past.

The City decided to exclude Brownies from the Division Church Parade in 1947, Guide recruits were allowed to attend the service but not to march. Also in 1947 the city quota, the fore-runner to the present census, was met by asking £1 from the larger districts of Headington, East and North and 10/- [50p] from South and West.

On Palm Sunday, 1947 there was a Guides' Own Service at the Sheldonian Theatre. A Guides' Own is a service by the Guides for the Guides and is particularly associated with camp. The Palm Sunday service refers only to Guides and only the Guide Law and Promise but it states that the opening words were by a Scouter.

In the Summer of 1947 1st Grimsbury Guides had their first camp away from Banbury:

Miss Wakelin hired someone with a furniture van to take us to Charnmouth in Dorset for two weeks. It was the first seaside

You *Edith Currill*
are now a RANGER.
Your duty is to LOOK WIDE and to
render SERVICE to others when and
where you can. God speed you in your efforts.

Olave Baden Powell.

Chief Guide

March 14' 1932

Above: *Edith Currill's Ranger Certificate signed by Lady B 1932.*

Right: *SRS Centaur, 1956.*

Below: *Ranger Service Star.*

Below, right: *Coronation Badge, 1937.*

holiday I ever had. By then my sister was a Guide so she came too. The weather was really nice and although some girls were very homesick we had a wonderful time.

Also in 1947, Lady Baden-Powell addressed PLs in the Sheldonian Theatre and talked to some of them in Broad Street afterwards.

1st Henley Guides all gave 1d [12d = 5p] to Princess Elizabeth's 21st birthday

In 1948 City Division sent out letters to prospective Trefoil Guild members and received 32 replies. The first meeting was held in Alma Hall (in East Oxford) on 28th January 1948. Quoted from the City minutes of 22nd January 1948:

Headquarters Finance

Miss Hobson reported the H.Q. required a permanent income and accordingly a suggestion had been put forward that at each meeting a Brownie should give an extra ha'penny and Guides and Rangers an extra 1d each. [one present penny = 2.5 old pennies]. *Half of the extra sum thus collected would go to H.Q. and half to a country and county fund. Commissioners were asked to discuss this idea with their districts. Miss Davenport suggested that H.Q. could earn some extra money by letting some of their rooms or by other forms of economy and this suggestion met with general approval. It was felt that Companies and Packs that paid large rents for their meeting place might find any additional subscription too much of a burden.*

In October 1947 the 2nd Witney Court of Honour minutes reports that:

... Petty Cash received from subs etc amounted to 7s-4d and the Camp Petty Cash was 11/-. A Voluntary Increase in Subscriptions of 2d a week was suggested as 1d does not pay its way.

[10/- = 50p; 2d is less than 1p]

Nothing new is there? We still grumble about the Census money and always have done so.

In February the City Guides joined with the Scouts for a Youth Night at the Town Hall as part of Silver Lining week. No Brownies were allowed to take part, only Guides and Rangers and the participating Guides had to be patrol leaders and preferably First Class. They were told to wear brown shoes.

In March the City Trefoil Guild was launched with 36 at the first meeting. The City Guild is still flourishing, in 1998 they celebrated with a 50th birthday party.

The members were strongly against wearing armlets but would like a special badge.

In March 1947, the City Division Court of Honour agreed that tinned food sent by Canadian Guides should be distributed to Guides camping or hiking to Beanwood. We learn that on the 10th June, HQ required 3/- for Guides and Rangers and 1/6 for Brownies per year for the next three years. [3/- = 15p]. Guiders were not required to pay.

Miss Wakelin formed a Ranger Unit

I remember going on the train either to Heyford or Somerton to be enrolled as a Ranger in the Village Hall with other girls from the area.

Extra clothing coupons were available from the Board of Trade for 'essential replacements' of uniform for Brown Owls and Captains. In April 1949 the County minutes record that each Division should receive an allocation of three clothing coupons per head based on the 1947 census figures, there were lots of forms to fill in to obtain these coupons!

The Commissioners in the City decided not to accept an invitation to a meeting in the Town Hall to organise help for families with influenza. It was thought that Guides would help families without the need of outside organisation and anyway it would be unwise to send children into a household with influenza. 'Flu' was a very serious illness a few years ago.

In March 1949 the County Youth Office reported that there were no youth organisations at all in the Barton (Headington) Estate. Needless to say the Guides stepped in and began the search for both a leader and premises. By April a Guide company and a Brownie pack had been formed.

During 1949 Rangers set up a model camp site at the County Agricultural Show; a levy of 1d per head was for insurance against accidents on Guide activities; Miss Bowen was commissioned to create a propaganda poster asking for camp sites for Guides; in July the City gained a grant of £25 from the King George Jubilee Trust towards the debt incurred by the purchase of Alma Hall, in East Oxford. At about this time a City Land Ranger Unit met at Alma Hall in the Winter and cycled out to Beanwood in the Summer. They often did some decorating and minor repairs to the cottage when they were there - as do most of us!

A special directive in October stated that silk stockings could be worn with uniform providing they were the correct colour. Remember, nylon stockings were not readily available and silk stockings were very expensive. Before this directive lisle stockings were worn with uniform, thick, thick St Trinians' stockings. Tights appeared much later.

Also in October every company and pack were warned that they were to be asked to provide a cake of soap for the delegates to next year's World Conference to be held in Oxford. City Division were asked to provide accommodation for 60 Aides. Guides would be used at the information centre at the Conference and University Scouts and Guides would conduct sight-seeing tours of the City.

References begin to appear to the creation of a County Standard, probably inspired by the dedication of the English Standard at Windsor in September. A meeting for the embroiderers of the County Standard was to be arranged.

The assorted activities in the 40s shows the determination of the Guide Movement both to help the war effort and to train girls and

Take us good Lord into Thy keeping, Guard us this

night while we are sleeping; Our praise to Thee we'll

daily in-crease, And till the morning light grant us Thy

peace, — And till the morning light grant us Thy peace.

THE OXFORD VESPER

TAKE US, GOOD LORD,

INTO THY KEEPING,

GUARD US THIS NIGHT

WHILE WE ARE SLEEPING,

OUR PRAISE TO THEE

WE'LL DAILY INCREASE

AND 'TILL THE MORNING LIGHT

GRANT US THY PEACE -

AND 'TILL THE MORNING LIGHT

GRANT US THY PEACE.

*Words and music
written by Janet Titchmarsh,
a young Guider in Oxford,
during a rest hour in camp
in the late 1940s.*

young women. As far as possible normal Guide activities took place while Good Turns associated with the war were completed. The country was struggling to find its feet, food was rationed, there were shortages of most things, there had been deaths and horrible injuries, no family was unscathed - but Oxfordshire Guides were looking forward to a County Standard and a World Conference.

* * * * * * * * * * * * * * * *

She forgot her hat! That's the sort of devil child she was!

We had to examine every jam jar for the Ministry of Food sign, we had to reject those without it. My sister and I went round the streets with a push-chair and a wheelbarrow.

The trainer said to buy a pair of boots that cost £40, more than my husband earned in a week! She told me I should leave my four sons at home when I camped. How could I?

My mother made us banana sandwiches. It was years before I discovered that those wartime banana sandwiches were made with parsnips.

Camp Sites

Beanwood, the County Camp Site, is a secluded and beautiful place, part of the Wytham Estate.

Colonel ffennell was a philanthropist from South Africa who bought Wytham Abbey and Estate, he gave his South African home to be a hospital for sick children. He was married with a daughter, Hazel, who died as a young woman. Colonel ffennel was, in effect, the Squire of Wytham village which, at that time, was in Berkshire.

When the ffennells first came to Wytham the Abbey was not ready for them and they camped in the grounds at The Follies site. This was a luxury affair with big tents on carpeted, wooden floors, staffed with of servants, not quite the Guide idea of camp. After they moved into the Abbey the tents were dismantled but the camp site, with wooden huts as solid shelter, was offered to the Guides.

The Follies were Swiss Chalet buildings at Wytham. From the elevated position we could see all over Oxford and, coincidentally (and usefully), hear the air raid sirens. Our air raid shelter was under the Chalet where they stored the hay for the cows, who also slept and did other things there. Colonel ffennel provided Dutch clogs as suitable footwear for 'playing' out of doors but we didn't use these. To get to the Follies and later Beanwood we had to walk, pulling trek carts in relays. We were very cross to leave The Follies for Beanwood which was not only much further to walk but, we then thought, a real dump.

After Hazel died, Colonel ffennell decided to make sure his property was used as he wished after his death. Hill End had been used for holidays for London shop girls, he decreed it was to be used for town children to learn to appreciate the countryside, it is now used by the LEA; the Abbey and the woods were to go to the University; permanent campsites were to be given to the

4th Cowley with evacuees at The Follies, 1942.

East Oxford Guides with their trek cart at The Follies, 1942.

Scouts and the Guides, these latter gifts were to be inviolate as long as the sites were used. This trust came into effect in 1947. The Guides still have the Beanwood site with the gamekeeper's Willow Cottage and the well; the Scouts were hounded out of their campsite by a farmer who insisted on ploughing the access.

Colonel ffennell's widow published Hazel's biography, in it is a photograph of Hazel and her friends having a snowdrop party on the grass apron in front of Willow Cottage, at that time the cottage was thatched. There are still, every year, carpets of snowdrops in the grass and in the woods as well as masses of bluebells in Beanwood itself.

The Guides first accessed their site through Hill End and the wood, then through Oaken Holt when it belonged to the Westminster Bank, now they use the Hill End access again, unfortunately there is limited car parking at Hill End. There have been problems with access and with impure water in the well but Beanwood remains a beautiful and peaceful site, well loved by those of us who learned our camping there. It was close enough to the city to trek out for a weekend and it was fully equipped, with chemical toilets in the woodshed. The cottage was thatched when it became ours, now it has been replaced with corrugated iron. The building is very attractive. That is the background to Beanwood, in a nutshell, but it is obvious through the County minutes and the camping minutes that it was not as simple as it sounds.

May 1929   The County Secretary read to the County Executive the reply from Colonel ffennell regretting the County's inability to accept his offer of a permanent campsite.

November 1929   The CCA received a further letter from the Colonel offering a permanent campsite at Felbury. The Executive decided on a visit to view the site.

May 1930   Miss Allen, CCA, reported on the difficulties that had arisen in connections with Colonel ffennell's offer of a

Both taken at The Follies 1938.

campsite. She was given permission to refuse or accept the offer after seeing the Colonel.

May 1932   The County minutes have a reference indicating that the camp site Colonel ffennell had been offering was the Follies. It was rejected again as the standing camp at Kirtlington Park was sufficient for 'camping requirements'. The Follies certainly was used as a camping site and was very reluctantly relinquished for Beanwood.

February 1938   A report to the Executive stated that Colonel ffennell had good camping sites and it was hoped these would be used.

January 1939   The Wytham sites had been used a great deal last year, a permanent campsite was again discussed.

While all this was going on there was also discussion about a campsites on Shotover, the woodland between Headington and Wheatley. In 1931 a reference is made to a camp site given by Mrs Miller who lived at Shotover House.

Westhill Farm was, we think, owned by the Oxford Preservation Trust and lent to Youth Movements for outdoor pursuits. In 1937 the County minutes record that the OPT wanted the co-operation of the Guides in making a site on Shotover a permanent camp site. This could have been Westhill Farm.

Westhill Farm? It was on the slopes of Shotover on the Horspath side. I remember going there with the Guides. I think it was a cook-out.

It was not a working farm and it had a resident Warden who lived in the old farmhouse. Westhill Farm is on present OS maps. Permission to visit the site had to be sought from an employee of the City Engineer's Office.

The Warden didn't like Scouts much.

The Highfield Guides (Headington) used to go to Westhill Farm for such things as the second class fire-lighting-with-only-two-matches - and no firelighters! Before that, in the first years of the '40s Air Scouts of the 8th Highfield frequently went to Westhill Farm. They used the big barn for some years and built an open fireplace there and they often flew model 'planes as did the Headington Rangers. The Rovers (present day Venture Scouts) had a den in the old stables.

I met David at Westhill Farm, I went with the Headington Rangers and he with the Air Scouts.

Margaret and David are happily married.

During the latter years of the war the site was little used, the Scout leaders were called up to fight and gradually the site was abandoned by Scouts but in April 1948 the City Division minutes record that Westhill Farm was going to be made into a proper camping place. The minutes relate that it had been lent to the Youth Organisations of Oxford and Guides, with a uniformed adult, could hike there and fires could be lit in the centre of the yard, Brownies could use the site. Wood and water were available. Westhill Farm is no longer used by Guides and Scouts.

In the County minutes references are made to two sites on Shotover that were abandoned in 1949 due to lack of water. There is also a reference in 1940 that nothing had been done about the site at Shotover because of a military firing range within 5 miles, there was a range at Brasenose Driftway At the moment it is unclear how many Shotover sites there were and which minute applies to which site.

The camp sites saga continues:

<u>1943</u> A list of equipment available at Eynsham and Beanwood was tabled along with proposed hiring rates. During the year 14 camps had been held at Beanwood. The cottage had suffered a break in and blankets and tins of fruit had been stolen. The windows were to be made more secure.

<u>1944</u> The County minutes record that the University Chest had confirmed that the Oxfordshire GGA could use

110

Beanwood indefinitely for camping with permission to enter Cowbarge copse for games under supervision.

Beanwood was booked for the entire season - well into September. This year 34 camps were held there.

<u>1945</u> Miss Bowen, CCA, was asked to cost the thatch repairs to the cottage before the Winter.

<u>1946</u> The estimate for re-thatching the cottage was £65, work was to begin shortly

<u>1954</u> The roof of the cottage at Beanwood is in need of repair. This time the thatch was replaced with green corrugated iron, less beautiful but more affordable.

<u>c1955</u> *I remember the well at Beanwood was contaminated. I always developed a terrible cough after Beanwood and I noticed other people did as well. The Camping committee refused to do anything so I, a young lieutenant, wrote to the Berkshire Health Committee (Beanwood was in Berkshire but was the Oxfordshire County camp site). The well was analysed and declared impure. The report came to me and I had to confess what I had done. The CAs spent a day scrubbing out the brick walls of the well but it was still analysed as unsafe. After that water was boiled and drinking water was fetched from Oaken Holt and another well was dug further up the field but that was not a success. I think I did right to take matters into my own hands but I was very unpopular.*

While we still use Beanwood it is remote and some companies find it scary, also there is a real problem with the water and the access, there is a telephone there, now. It remains a popular camp site, the Senior Section hold camps there as well as Guides; Brownies hold revels; the Warblers sing there; Trefoil Guilds hold cookouts. There are a number of visits to Beanwood at both snowdrop and bluebell times.

In July 1951 a camp at Beanwood, attended by Guides from Chesterton, Bicester, Islip, Stoke-Lyne and Tusmore, is recorded in Joy Fowler's personal log:

... at camp-fire ... Jill Burrows gave us some of her lovely poems ... one of which was about 'Beanwood':

Beanwood Camp

Way amongst hilltops, fields and trees
Where the birds sing a tune to the waft of the breeze
Lies Beanwood Camp for Rangers and Guides
A place where goodness and friendship abides

Beanwood is a happy world on its own
It's quiet and peaceful and all alone
When we reach Beanwood our cares flee away
Our hearts feel much lighter, happier, gay

There's a quaint old cottage and a wishing well
And leafy green woods where the fairies dwell
We travel each morn through those dewy woods
To fetch our milk and other goods

So if you feel dull or out of sorts
And lacking the company of jolly good sports
Come to Beanwood for Rangers and Guides
A place where goodness and friendship abides

A much more recent quote from a Trefoil Guild member:

Shotover Trefoil went to Beanwood one lovely June evening. Eileen and I were volunteered to cook the sausages. We were going, as Guides, to a Buckingham Palace Garden Party the next day and our friends thought we should keep our feet firmly on the ground! It took half the night to get the smell of smoke out of my hair.

The Garden Party was wonderful, it was a perfect day. HQ let us titivate there and kept open late so we could collect our coats. Our invitations came through the Lord Lieutenant.

* * * * * * * * * * * * * * * *

We were entitled to one third of a pint of milk for school age children when in camp. This was the school milk allocation which was available for groups of children on holiday. It came in ordinary bottles, we did not have to cope with crates of small bottles.

There was a wood fired boiler in the cottage, brick built, a large affair. We used it for hot water. It was not easy to light the fire underneath the boiler.

In the lat sheeted were piles and piles of gadget wood. Beanwood had a lot of hazel bushes which are absolutely ideal for gadgets. Before our Summer camp we used to go to Beanwood and go gadget wooding in the wood between Hill End and our field (Beanwood).

We were allowed to use the Hill End swimming pool.

Senior Section, Trefoil Guild and Hospitals

The Senior Section consisted of Land Rangers, usually called Rangers, Sea Rangers, Air Rangers and Cadets. Cadets were being trained as Guide Leaders, they wore white ties, a white band on their hats and a white enamelled badge.

The first known Cadet unit was the 1st North Oxford Unit which was opened in 1921, closed in '22 and re-registered in 1926. On 1st June 1924, 2nd Headington Cadets were formed, they were registered on 18th November. In '36/'37 Oxford City Division Cadet Unit was registered. A County Cadet Unit was in existence c1963, it was run as a post unit. Cadets were replaced by the Young Leader Scheme.

A Ranger Unit was formed in 1917, 6th Oxford YWCA Rangers, in 1923 Miss Stavely and Miss Stace, neither warranted, ran the 3rd Headington Ranger Patrol. This became 3rd Headington Rangers then Headington Rangers. In 1931, 5th Headington (Wingfield Hospital) Rangers were formed only to be disbanded in 1932.

We know of several Sea Ranger units:

SRS Vindictive, registered 1932   (SRS = Sea Ranger Ship)
SRS Foudroyant, 1935
SRS Nubian
SRS King George V, 1941   (disbanded 1953)
SRS Terra Nova, Warborough, 1945.
SRS Artful, Chipping Norton, 1954   (disbanded 1955)

In the 1964 the East Oxford minutes recorded that the Sea Rangers had disbanded and their boat sold for £5. The next year the £5 was given to Mrs Beresford for the Open Company of Land, Sea and Air Rangers. There was a Sea Ranger Company in Henley, the leaders of the Henley unit and SRS Nubian served in the GIS.

Oxford Sea Rangers were started by Miss Dorothea Smith with SRS Foudroyant, Ruth Denton was 'Mate'. The second crew, SRS Nubian was still running in 1944. SRS Nubian built a sailing dinghy which was on the water in 1961.

We do not have many memories from our Senior Section but those to whom I have spoken remember their days as Rangers or Cadets with pleasure, reckoning their days in the Senior Section were their happiest Guide days.

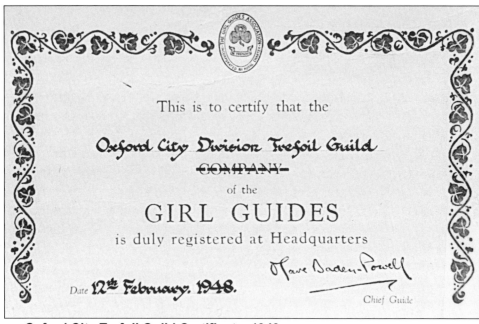

This is to certify that the

Oxford City Division Trefoil Guild

~~COMPANY~~

of the

GIRL GUIDES

is duly registered at Headquarters

Olave Baden-Powell

Date **12th February, 1948.**

Chief Guide

Oxford City Trefoil Guild Certificate, 1948.

Queen's Guide Award and First Class Badge.

Old Guides, Guidons, Trefoil Guild

As far back as the 1920s there had been unofficial groups of Old Guides, usually linked to the Companies in which they had been Guides. In 1936 the Oxfordshire CC, Mrs Evelyn Mason, asked Divisions for lists of Ex-Guides, Rangers and Guiders. She explains that Guidons are an experiment and she wants Oxfordshire to participate. The notice goes on to explain that Guidons should be self-supporting, not taking leaders from the Movement. Local groups should join with Guide activities in their area. Membership is open to all who have made the Promise and are prepared to live by it. They must have been enrolled in the Movement for at least a year. In 1936 the title 'World Order of Guides' was proposed as a possible title instead of Guidons, which indicated that the members had 'gone on' in Guiding.

1937 - Miss Saunderson was appointed County Recorder for Old Guides, this was not a HQ appointment. In 1938 Miss Sanderson reported there were 27 old Guides. The Trefoil Guild was mentioned for the first time in 1943 - and shelved. Miss Jeffery reported in 1944 that it had been decided to have a joint Post Trefoil Guild with Berkshire.

In 1945 the question was - should we have a County Trefoil Guild? Possibly with one in Banbury as well. Bullingdon Trefoil Guild was registered in 1947 but disbanded two years later. In 1948 Oxford City Guild was opened with 36 members, the subscription was 2/6d a year (less than 13p). It is still a prospering Guild and a second Guild now operates in the City and a dozen or so others in the County. Vexing question were whether the Guild members should wear armbands? Was the Trefoil Guild meeting the needs of Rangers? Was it meeting often enough? Armbands were emphatically rejected.

The Oxford City Guild sent a potted history for this book:

The inaugural meeting of the Guild was held at Alma Hall on Wednesday, 28th January 1948. ... one of the Foundation members was Mrs Sue Moles who is now our President. [1998] *... the format that is still followed today - 8 indoor meetings and 4 outdoor ones. ... at Wesley Memorial Hall ... by the 1949 AGM there were 46 members. ... In 1977 Miss Mollie Axtell designed and made a cloth for the meeting room table, to be used for the 30th Birthday on 12th February 1978. It is still in use today. ... 1986 when numbers began to fall due to bus services being cut back and the older members not wanting to go out in the evenings ... changed to Monday afternoons in September 1988. From then on the Guild started to grow again ...*

and - in November 1988 a second Guild was formed in the city, Shotover, an evening Guild, for those not wanting to go into the City and for those still working.

Nowadays Trefoil Guilds are flourishing, they do not wear uniform but there are badge tabs - bright red - polo-shirts and sweat-shirts with logos and County names. Most Guilds meet once a month and most meet out of doors in the Summer. Men or women can be enrolled into the TG, most members are long term Guides. Some members help units on a permanent basis, some would help In an emergency. TGs help within the County and their own areas with badge testing; trainers' lunches; preparation of rooms; registration at trainings; teas and coffees; squash and biscuits. Guilds help at Brownie Revels; Jumble Sales; they make cakes for cake stalls; they have parties and invite other Guilds. They have their own meetings with speakers and demonstrations; they go out for meals or to throw boomerangs and fly kites; they have cook-outs and barbecues; garden parties and tree planting; picnics and walks; learn handbells and macrame; watch videos of the Police Helicopter in action; visit Fire Stations, Foxlease, Warwick Castle; Tesco's; go bowling; whatever one can think of a Guild somewhere has done it or is planning to do it. Most of all, they are there, ready to help when needed. In the last few years Trefoil Guild members over 55 have been taking part in the Dark Horse Venture. For this they are learning new skills, taking on new responsibilities, helping others, not necessarily Guides, on a regular basis. In 1999 we have Gold awards in the County.

Guild members also do Good Turns, a sample taken from Oxford City Guild across 50 years:

sending clothes to refugees during and after World War 2;

adopting a Displaced family and kitting them out with new underclothes as they prepared to emigrate to America;

forming a rota to push the wheelchairs and bath chairs of Guides in the Wingfield Hospital, taking them to their meetings or therapy sessions;

sending gifts and visiting Dr Barnado children;

visiting a nun and two residents in St John's Home (a nursing home attached to a convent), taking the Trefoil Magazine and keeping them in touch;

visiting and taking out a Spastic Guide and occasionally bringing her, in her wheelchair, to Guild meetings.

knitting tiny baby clothes for premature baby unit.

The name of this section of Guiding has been contentious, even now there is talk of changing our name.

* * * * * * * * * * * * * * * *

My Trefoil Guild friends supported me through a time of great difficulty. My husband was always a little scornful of Guiding but before he died I heard him tell a friend that there was something in this Guide thing, his wife's Guide friends had been marvellous and he was sure they would continue to help her after his death. They did.

One husband to another at a Guide function:
'Listen to the noise, it sounds like an aviary. In a moment my wife will raise her hand in the air and there will be silence within seconds.'
There was - total silence.

Above: *1st Cowley Guides, the Poplars Poor Law School Company, 1936.*

Right: *A Lone enrolment badge with an L across it.*

Below: *East District Rangers entertaining Post and Lone Guides, 1934.*

Posts and Lones

In the 20s there were several extra-ordinary units.
Two Post Guide Companies were formed in the County, these companies were for girls who could not attend Guide meetings because of health problems. The two companies were the 1st Oxfordshire Post Guide Company, and the 2nd Oxfordshire Wingfield Post Guide Company. The Wingfield Hospital is now the Nuffield Orthopaedic Centre. These units were started in 1925 and registered in 1926.
One lady has tells how she was a patient in the Wingfield Hospital for nine months and was a Guide in hospital. At that time Orthopaedic complaints, especially for children, entailed months of treatment and months lying flat in bed or in basketwork beds on wheels for occasional outings. The girls wore their Guide ties, badges and hats over their night-clothes for meetings. They loved the Drumhead Services, they were pushed out in their beds while the rest of us marched into the hospital grounds with flags flying. The Services were organised by the Scouts but included the Guides. After her recovery the lady remembers going to Mrs Teal's house in Iffley to learn bedmaking and going to the Poor Law School, (The Poplars) in Cowley to learn First Aid. In 1934 the two Post companies were combined, the Wingfield Guides becoming the 1st Oxon Post Company. Nowadays very few are hospitalised for long periods and if they are they are too ill for Guides.
In 1923 the 1st Oxon Lones were formed under the leadership of Miss James de Trafford. Lones were for Guides living in lonely places or in schools where Guides were forbidden There was a 'meeting' by post which each Guide received and answered. She would send in her reef knot and her Second Class useful article and it would be returned with comments with the next meeting letter. The 1st Adderbury Lone Patrol was formed in

1923 and disbanded in 1946. Today's Guides can usually get to meetings and very few schools and institutions refuse to have a Guide Unit and so the need for Lones no longer exists.

A University Club

The first mention of the University Scout and Guide Club is in 1929. The Club is still active . The club is for members of the University who wish to keep up their Scouting and Guiding links. This club has been a source of temporary leaders and of organisers of Brownie Revels and such like.

The Poor Law School

There were Guides and Brownies at the Poplars, the Poor Law school in Cowley.
I remember there were Brownies. And Scouts. They were allowed to camp and we were not. There weren't any Guides. There must have been Guides, I was in the Violet Patrol! We wore a grey uniform to school, St Christopher's, which marked us out. I was happy at the Poplars, the girls had a good training in domestic duties, it was more or less expected that we would be servants.'
There was a least one Ranger, presumably a Lone or Post Ranger, in The Laurels, the workhouse in Headington. We have found references to Guides in Headington taking turns to take her out in her wheelchair on Sunday afternoons.
I asked a dear lady in Cowley, a much loved Brown Owl a few years ago, if she remembered anything about the Poplars Company and Pack - whether the girls joined District or Division events, Church Parades or anything else. Her eyes glazed over as she chanted:
> *Headington kids are jolly good kids*
> *But Cowley kids are better!*

It seems that when Headington, Headington Quarry, Hockmore, Church Cowley and Temple Cowley were separate villages and hamlets outside the City of Oxford there was little love lost between the settlements. The lady was over 80 but she remembered that rhyme from kindergarten days, when she was my father's best girl-friend.

The Oxford Gang Show

When Gang Shows began in 1932 there were rumblings about it being an all male preserve but that is the way Ralph Reader wrote the Shows. Female Scout Leaders and Guides of all ages were disappointed at being excluded. In 1967 girls were admitted to Venture Scout units. This led to more discontent, if girls could be Venture Scouts why could they not be in a Show? Ralph Reader reluctantly agreed, in 1968, to allow females in the London Gang Show - but he imposed conditions. They had to be of Venture age and were restricted to a dance team. This was later extended. There are still some all-male Shows but Oxford is not one of them. Now, of course, Brownies are also in the Gang.

In the Spring of 1950 the Oxfordshire Scout Association performed a musical play by Ralph Reader, 'We'll Live Forever', for four performances. It was estimated that 1,000 people saw that production, it was the beginning of the Oxford Gang Show. In 1951 a show was held in the Town Hall, Oxford. It was not a Gang Show as such, it was a Display by the local Scout Association. Included were songs by Ralph Reader and Guides and Rangers took part. The rehearsals were at Magdalen College School, we sat on apparatus type benches, it was probably the gymnasium. In 1998 two ladies old enough to know better, having had the memory sparked by research for this book, sang to each over the 'phone:

Sta-ar of the e-e-vening, pretty little evening sta-a-ar

123

One was a Guide, the other a Ranger in 1951. Neither of us could remember anything else from the show, neither could remember the show itself, only the rehearsal.

The Gang Show moved venue several times and in 1967 they were invited to perform for the Lord Mayor's Old Folks Christmas Party in Oxford's Town Hall. 10th Oxford (Marston) Guides and 43rd Oxford Scouts presented a one hour programme of songs which was popular. This engagement was repeated on 1968 and 1969. In 1970 the Oxford Scout and Guide Show was performed in the Town Hall.

The admission of the females gave the Show a greater scope and flexibility which was further improved by the creation, in 1972, of the Junior Gang, formed of Brownies and Cubs. The Show moved to the Polytechnic College in Headington in 1972 and over 2,500 tickets were printed. Attendances improved year on year and a larger venue became necessary. 1975 saw the Gang have the honour of giving the first ever public performance in St Edward's School new theatre.

In 1978 capacity was still a problem and the New Theatre (now the Apollo) was the only place big enough to cope with the Show's popularity. Unfortunately neither Guide nor Scout County Associations were prepared to finance the Show and required a 'bond' to cover any loss. The bond money was given by cast members and supporters and the Show gave four performances to ~7,500 people. The Theatre provided an opportunity to increase cast numbers. In 1981 the Show ran for five nights and in 1984 for a full week.

Profit is not the main function of the Gang Show - in 1996 the profit was £200 - but it plays a part. The Show has given money to Jubilee House, Leader Training, Youlbury, etc, any profit being shared equally between the two Associations. The Sing-a-Long raises money for local charities.

To quote the current Gang Show Committee Chairman :

The essential ingredient of the Gang Show is spirit - a determination to continue and improve whatever the problems ... One problem is that each year the standard of the youngsters rises, it is a pity we have to refuse so many.
The Gang Show is still very much alive in Oxford, the Apollo Theatre is packed for a week every March and on one evening the Chain Gang attend - that is an affectionate nick-name for the local dignitaries many of whom wear beautiful chains of office.

* * * * * * * * * * * * * * * *

One Guide Company borrowed a commode from the Red Cross on the days they entertained disabled Guides from the Workhouse.

My daughter was in the Gang Show while her 'mock' GCEs were in progress. I met her from school, she showered, changed, I took her to the theatre picking up two Guides and a Scout from various points in Cowley - and fetched her at night. She knew we disapproved, as did her headmistress but she proved us wrong and did well in her exams.

I fetched my Young Leader daughter and her non-Scout boy friend from the post-performance party at 5am.

A Gang Show picture.

and More . . .

The early 50s were exciting times to be a young Guide in Oxfordshire - I know, I was one and I lived through history.

The 13th World Conference of Girl Guides and Girl Scouts was held in Oxford from July 1950

In 1949 a sub-committee was appointed from the County Court of Honour to deal with local arrangements for the World Conference to be held in Oxford in 1950. The committee members were the County Commissioner and Secretary; Miss Hobson; Miss Bowen; Miss Allen; Miss Tallon Brown; Miss Christie-Miller; Mrs Lee.

Oxfordshire were asked to put on an entertainment each evening, the challenge was accepted. The Local Association was asked to give an extra donation. Every company and pack in the County provided a cake of toilet soap for the delegates. Kidlington Rangers painted 150 jam jars to hold flowers in the delegates' rooms. There was to be a party at Blenheim Palace for Commissioners and Presidents.

Sunday, 16th July was designated Guide Sunday by the GGA and a special form of Service was printed for use in Churches. Many Guides went to Church in uniform that Sunday and many more held Guides' Own Services. The following extract from the 3rd Abingdon Guide Company Log Book No 5 gives an idea of what happened. At the time Abingdon was in Berkshire but is now in Oxfordshire.

This day was set apart for us to prayer (sic) for 40 years of Guiding and for guidance to those who will be attending the World Conference at Oxford in July.

5th East Oxford Guides with the Motor road Scroll.

Many of us went to church in uniform and in the afternoon we had a Guides' Own Service at 120 Oxford Road.

Only 8 Guides were able to get to this service but those who came thought it worth the while to pray and sing together for an hour. We started our Guides' Own in Captain's garden but rain came on so we moved into the garage and continued our service there. We sang some of our favourite hymns and prayers we had chosen and some from the leaflet prepared for Guide Sunday. Captain spoke to us on our need for friendship with all Guides, starting with our own patrol, until we would spread friendliness through the world.

The Order of Service issued by the GGA includes prayers for the Royal Guides (the Princesses Elizabeth and Margaret), prayers for Lady Baden-Powell, thanksgiving for the inspiration of Lord Baden-Powell and a prayer for the delegates to the World Conference. The Service included the carrying of Colours, the Promise and the National Anthem.

The Conference was held at St Hugh's College, Oxford, and was opened by the Princess Royal, our British President. At that time there were two and a half million Guides. The theme of the Conference was 'This Changing World'.

During the week of the Conference several activities were planned and local Guides had a wonderful time. There was a Water Pageant on the River Cherwell, in the University Parks. The VIPs had seats on the city side of the river, the Guides and the general public were on the Marston side. The Pageant was staged on a series of punts which floated along the river to Handel's Water Music. Rangers acted as Life Guards, patrolling the pageant in a punt. The 2nd Witney Guides' Minutes report:

Our Company took part in the water Pageant at Oxford, under the title of "Swan Upping".

A series of Scrolls of Friendship were brought from all over

Wheatley and Thame Guides at a Scroll change-over point.

Abingdon Guides also at a change-over point.

the country, by various means of transport, to Oxford where they were brought to the Broad Walk in Christchurch Meadows. Queen's Guides or First Class Guides carried the scrolls to the camp fire at Headington where they were distributed to delegates to take back to their countries.

For example, the Scroll for Brazil travelled by the green paths of England, passed from hand to hand, until on 29 July it was presented to the Commissioners for England, Scotland and Wales in the Broad Walk of Christchurch Meadows, Oxford, from whence it went to the Camp Fire at Headington and was presented to the delegate from Brazil.

One Scroll came by motor route, one by river, one on horse-back - all 27 arrived safely in the Meadows. The Scrolls passed through Counties and Districts and each was escorted from one change-over point to the next. The Ceremony in the Meadows was exciting, first the Colours were paraded through the Memorial Gardens then the Scrolls came, by their various transports, along the Broad Walk. Obviously, some of the means of transport had to be improvised, no 'plane could land in the Meadows and the river does not run along the Broad Walk, but the parade was colourful and interesting nonetheless - the motor transport Scroll came in a slow-moving car with Guides clinging to the outside and flanked by Guides in pedal cars.

Another example - Grimsbury Guides helped to collect three Scrolls: from Stratford-on-Avon by canal; from Warwick by cycle, taking it from Edge Hill to Bloxham; one on foot at Blacklocks Hill from Northampton. Queen's Guide Myra Bessevy presented a Scroll and book to Princess Margaret.

On the Saturday of the camp fire 5th East Oxford Guides held an open-air canteen outside their HQ, near the Plain. They were strategically placed on the way from the City Centre to Headington and the canteen was advertised in *The Guide* and was very busy all that Saturday.

Captain said that only second class Guides could help with the canteen. I worked jolly hard to finish my second class! The campfire at Cheney Lane, in Headington, was attended by over ten thousand Guides and was a wonderful occasion. Miss Deeley and Miss Logan were the organisers and Miss Mary Chater was the leader. Princess Margaret attended as did the Princess Royal, Guides came from all over the country. During the camp fire 'sparks' flew, enamelled paper discs of the world badge, many of the ten thousand Guides secured a 'spark'. All the VIP guests were presented with a spark, Ruth Cox from 5th East Oxford Company presented a 'spark' to Princess Margaret. During this camp fire the Scrolls of Friendship were presented to the national delegates. The proceedings were broadcast on the radio, Miss Chater held a short practice before the guests arrived to make sure the microphones were picking up the singing.

It is hard to describe my feelings as I sat on the grass that evening, a part of the horseshoe of 10,000 Guides. For the first time I felt a part of the family of Guides that I had heard about but had not been able to imagine.

I stood, awe-stricken, as the members of the World Association walked through the gangways left open between the Guides. The procession of flags was stunning, the World Flag led, followed by the national flags of all the participating countries. First they marched down the centre gangway and then the national flags divided and were carried up the side gangways and round the outside to flank the horseshoe. The representatives of each country were greeted with cheers from the excited Guides. HRH the Princess Margaret came into the arena with the World Chief Guide, Lady Baden-Powell and the Imperial HQ Commissioner, the Lady Stratheden and Campbell. I could have touched the Princess had I moved my hand slightly outward - but Captain would not have been pleased so my hand stayed by my side.

After a welcome by the Princess and an inspiring talk from the Chief, specially chosen Oxfordshire Guides came running down the gangways with the Scrolls and presented them to Princess Margaret, each one making a short speech telling us from where the scroll had come, how it had travelled and where it was going. Each of the 27 National Delegates walked up to receive her Scroll - it was so colourful - each delegate was in National costume and each curtsied to the Princess as she received her country's scroll and the logbook that detailed its journey through Britain.

The fire was lit and 'Camp Fire's Burning' swelled through the evening - I am a Grandmother now but tears come to my eyes as I remember the pride I felt that evening, pride in my uniform (and my new second class badge on my sleeve), pride in the Movement to which we all belonged. We sang through the programme, which was broadcast on the wireless, and as the fire died we sang Taps, the Chief Guide wished us Good Night and all that was left was to wait our turn to leave the field.

I went home inspired by a magical experience and I believe over 10,000 other Guides did so too.

We were privileged to be Oxfordshire Guides that Summer.

* * * * * * * * * * * * * * * * *

Do you remember - Miss Chater conducted the singing with a torch?

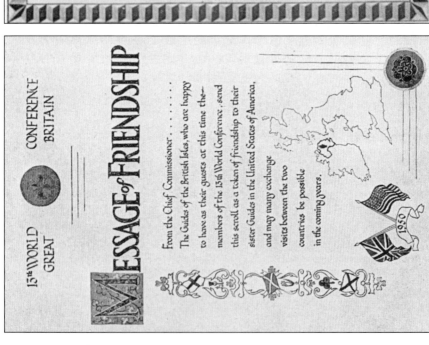

Examples of two of the Scrolls sent out from Oxford.
One is to the USA, the other to Belgium.

The County Standard

The Oxfordshire County Standard, still in use, was dedicated on 17 June 1951 at St Aldate's Church with an overflow service in St Mary's, both in Oxford City. Approximately one thousand members of the Movement attended the two services. We sang: Onward Christian Soldiers; All people that on earth do dwell; Love Divine all loves excelling; O Jesus, I have promised and, after the presentation of the Standard to the CC by the Rector of St Aldate's

Land of our birth, we pledge to Thee
Our love and toil in the years to be;
When we are grown and take our place
As men and women with our race.

(I quote the first verse only)

This hymn, sung with feeling and sincerity by so many young girls and women was appropriate to the occasion.

A march past was held in the Broad Walk of Christchurch Meadows with the County President, the Duchess of Marlborough, taking the salute, the County Standard was carried by Queen's Guides. Banbury and Kidlington Rangers were the first to carry the new Standard at a Ranger Rally.

The story of the Standard began in 1945 when the County Minutes record that it was agreed to see if the 2nd Henley Standard could be converted into a County Standard. In 1949 the minutes indicate that a sub-committee was formed and various designs for a Standard submitted. Each Division, there were then five, designed its own motif and a team of needlewomen, led by Mrs Gosset worked on the Standard while Mrs Vaughan, Division Commissioner for North Oxfordshire, consulted the Heraldry College. Miss Deeley"s Rangers made the case; the pole and trefoil badge to surmount it were ordered. In December 1950 it was

Above:
*Our
Standard.*

Right:
*East Oxford
Guiders at
Foxlease,
1952.*

reported that the cost was £36 15s 0p [15/- = 75p] with £3 or £4 still owing on the pole and trefoil.

The embroidery was completed by volunteers from all over the County, each Guider placed at least one stitch. The five motifs were: Oxford City, the lion on the battlements; North, A Lady on a White Horse for Banbury; South, Old Father Thames for Henley; East, Dorchester Abbey; West, sheep and blankets for Witney. The trefoil is self-explanatory as is the motto 'Be Prepared'. Audeo, meaning 'I dare' comes from the motto of the then County Commissioner, Lady Rose, and the arms of the Earls of Macclesfield The Ox on its Ford is from Oxfordshire County Council's heraldic badge. Mrs Vaughan designed the Standard using the Division-designed motifs and she was the Standard bearer for the dedication.

More Divisions were created but the Standard was not changed. When the Berkshire Divisions came into Oxfordshire there was discussion about adding to the Standard but it was decided to leave it as it was. We now have eleven Divisions in the County. We are sentimentally attached to our County Standard and most of us do not want to change it.

* * * * * * * * * * * * * * * *

In 1951 there was a service in Ritz cinema for both Guides and Scouts. The stand of Colours is particularly remembered. Guide entries from Oxford were displayed at the Festival of Britain. On 21st June there was a City Division Rally which attracted some criticism:

helpers should have been given tea;
companies should have supported the LA stall;
ground too big, numbers taking part in displays too few;
patrol corners not well set up;
more stewards needed;
loudspeaker van position should have been rehearsed.

A Guide remembers:

Right: *A Colour Party at the Rally on the Iffley Road Running Ground, 1951.*

Below: *Enrolment Badge of the time.*

Below: *Benson Guides at Epye, 1941.*

I remember the Division Rally, in the early fifties. It was on the Iffley Road Running Ground - that's where the first four-minute mile was run years later. We had displays of proficiency badges round the field, my patrol did Hiker Badge. At the opening, we were all sitting in a circle, over the loudspeaker came a voice asking the owner of a black Ford Popular registration number *** *** to move it as it was causing an obstruction. All our company knew it was Captain's car, I still know that number but I won't tell you. We watched with pride and sorrow as Captain walked, all alone, with everyone watching, out of the circle, across the running ground to the entrance. It seemed to be miles! Pride because our Captain had a car and sorrow that she was so very embarrassed.

In November an appeal for Guiders was published in the Oxford Times. Nothing changes does it?

A note in the Oxford City minutes for 1952 states that *'the Trefoil Guild will lend toddlers on Saturday afternoons for Child Nurse Badge'.* I wonder if they were the children or the grandchildren of the TG members? In the same year the City Trefoil adopted a Polish family.

Still in 1952 and with the City, it was stated that news may be sent to newspapers by Guiders but <u>not</u> letters, only Commissioners may write letters to the press.

There was an international camp at Hall Barn that year, a number of campers went from Oxfordshire and a number of Companies visited the camp for the traditional camp fire.

The Honourable Mrs Gibbs, in Clifton Hampden, held a lunch party for Oxfordshire Commissioners to meet the Lady Stratheden and Campbell in advance of the Hall Barn Camp. I was sent to help with the occasion as an Unexpected Job for my Queen's Guide, the old style Queen's Guide Award. There were four of us and we helped the servants. It was an experience! We helped the chamber maids make the beds, the cook to prepare food, the housemaid to answer the door and, the highlight, we helped the butler serve the meal. We had a crash course on the correct way to serve and clear, it was nerve-racking but the butler kept his eye on us. I think he was very good to tolerate us interfering with his duties. We helped to wash up, two of us with the kitchen maid and two in the Butler's Pantry doing glasses and silver.

When Guides from Chesterton, Bicester, Islip, Stoke-Lyne, and Tusmore camped at Beanwood the Guiders wasted no opportunity. Joy Fowler writes in her personal log:

Camp-fire was held in the evening after which B Wyatt, Vera and myself [Joy Fowler] *went to get some more gadget sticks and sat in the light of the camp-fire making wash stands.*

In 1952 the same log, at a camp at Broughton Castle the cows upset things for the 1st Chesterton Guides:

While we were waiting for it [supper] *the cows paid us another visit. Miss Wakelin chased them away which made the Guides laugh. Really they were rather a nuisance. Almost every night at about 5 o'clock in the morning they would come over amongst the tents and lats. On one occasion they nipped the screening of the lats, so we had to build a fence round collecting all the bits of string and rope we could find. This caused great fun.*

1st East outside St Mary and St John Church.

The Coronation - 1953

During 1952 and the beginning of 1953 plans were laid for the Coronation Rally to be held at Blenheim Palace in co-operation with the Scouts. It was stated that the Guides and Scouts were to contribute £25 from County funds, each, presumably, and that the public would be charged 1/- [5p] to attend. The Guide performance was to be from 2.30 - 4.30 and the Scouts from 4.30 - 6.30. The City Division thought the programme too long and referred this back to the Committee. The Guides were to arrive by midday with picnic lunches. Enquiries were to made as to whether a special train could be run between Oxford and Woodstock. In the event that train did run. Both LA and TG were to be involved in the Rally. Rehearsals for the displays and the camp fire for the Rally were held in Angel Meadow (by the Plain in Oxford) and on the University Running Ground.

At the start of the Rally the Guides ran out of the trees and down the slope to the front of the platform. At least one Guide leader did not enjoy that part of the Rally:

I remember feeling very foolish as we burst from the wooded bits and ran down the grassy slope.

A camp was erected in double quick time after the opening ceremony. Each unit portrayed a proficiency badge (as the badges were called then) in a static display.

I was at the point of taking over a Company and we decided to do Photographer Badge. I wrote to Ilford and they were very generous sending us posters , etc.

The Rally was a big success and very much enjoyed by the Guides themselves. For many of them it was to be the only time they would ever see The Chief Guide.

Yes, I remember the Rally. I was a Queen's Guide and was in the Guard of Honour for Lady B-P. There were twelve Queen's Guides and twelve Queen's Scouts, we lined up at

The run-in at Blenheim Palace, 1953.

Cowley Guides demonstrated Photographer's Badge at the Rally.

the approach to the platform, the Guides facing the Scouts. We came to attention and saluted and the Chief Guide walked between the lines and shook hands (left-handed) with each of the Guides, she then turned back to shake hands with the Scouts but by that time the Colour Party with her Standard and all the VIPS were right behind her and had to back up to allow her to go back to the beginning of the line again. It caused a bit of a kerfuffle but Lady B-P insisted.

The flags and standards were placed in stands on the platform after the opening but there was always a Colour Party with each one. Lady B-P, later on, shook hands, two at a time (her left hand to two Guiders' left hands, her right hand coming over to enclose the hands) with any Guider with whom she had not shaken hands in the past. There was a long queue but she spoke to each one.

The train was quite exciting, I believe the line and Woodstock station was re-opened for us, I remember particularly the level crossing just past the city boundary.

A Guide from Banbury carried the World Chief Guide's Standard at the Rally.

All this happened in Coronation Year and it was a busy year. The County sent Guides to the Coronation Service and to places along the route of the processions. There were Oxfordshire Guides at a Celebration Church Service in London. There was also a Coronation Tribute, each Division prepared a Tribute from a Ranger, Cadet, Commissioner, Company, Pack, Patrol, Guide and Brownie.

A combined Youth Service was held in the University Parks on 31st May 1953 with a rehearsal in Angel Meadow beforehand (under Magdalen Bridge).

Guides could wear a special embroidered Coronation badge from Thinking Day, 1953 to the end of the year and commercial biscuits were made with this badge embossed on them. A penny (an old penny, worth much less than the

Right: *Poster for the Rally.*

Below: *The 1953 Coronation Badge.*

Below: *Lady Rose, County Commissioner, presents three Queen's Guide Awards in East Oxford.*

Oxfordshire Scouts and Guides

invite YOU to a

GREAT
Coronation Rally

in

Blenheim Park, Woodstock

on

Saturday, JULY 18th, 1953

at 2.30 p.m.

Opened personally by

The Lady Baden-Powell.

Commentator: FREDDIE GRISEWOOD.

For details—ask your local Scout & Guide people

present penny) was given to the Movement for each packet sold. A profit of £10,000 was made over the whole country.

My mother bought only one packet of the Guide biscuits because neither of my brothers would eat them. They said a biscuit with a Guide badge on it made them sick.

A number of Companies sent messages of loyalty to the Queen through the traditional route, Commissioners onwards. These were on colourful cards and some tributes were sent to the Palace. The 1st Freeland Guides, as part of their tribute, Spring cleaned the Village Hall, planted and kept a garden in the centre of the village and collected Queen's Head pennies [old pennies with the head of the Queen Victoria on them]. Some of these pennies went to the Church and some were used for seeds and plants for the garden.

An International camp was held in Holland in Coronation Year. A Guide from 5th East Oxford, was chosen as one of two British Guides to attend. She recalls:

I did not possess a ruc-sac, I always used my late Uncle's RAF green canvas kitbag. I did have a groundsheet. Miss Staveley lent me her ruc-sac and I set off for London, alone, to meet a Guider and two Guides from Eire. I had to find my way to Our Ark, the predecessor to Pax Lodge. As well as normal camp kit I had to take a bowl for washing myself, and a Union Jack to carry. I was somewhat loaded, I had the ruc-sac on my back, I held the bedding roll in my hand, by its cord, the big Union Jack, which was very heavy, over one shoulder. I arrived by coach at Victoria Station and walked to Buckingham Palace Road, I remember asking a policeman the way. He recognised my uniform. I felt proud of myself when I finally arrived, I had not been out of Oxford alone before and had only visited London twice.

My mother saw me off from Oxford not knowing when I would return, we were told about three weeks. She was worried out of her mind, no one in the family had ever had a passport before and while proud of me, a Queen's Guide and chosen for this camp, I am sure she would have given a great deal to have been able to cancel the whole thing.

It all worked out well, it was a wonderful experience. First we went to a Guide Centre, then to the camp where I met Henny with whom I was to stay, then a week's hospitality. It was in Holland that I first tasted yoghurt, it was years before it came to England. I also tasted eels. Henny's family were very good to me and gave me a wonderful time. They sent me home with a food parcel and some cigars for my father. Although the Dutch suffered dreadfully in the war they had plenty of food in 1953 while in Great Britain we were still rationed and there were shortages. An innocent little romance occurred, Henny's older brother Han was rather nice. He came to England years later to see me but by that time I was married. He has never married.

The family were very kind to me. One day we cycled miles, Holland is flat so I managed, I had a bicycle with a back pedal brake and nearly killed myself. A car veered towards me, I instinctively swerved left, as I was riding on the right that was into the car's path, and groped for the brakes levers that were not there. Another day a car was hired to take me out and we had a puncture. Captain had taught me the theory of changing a car wheel as part of the preparation for my Queen's Guide Be Prepared Test. I was able to give instructions to Han and his father, neither of whom had any idea of changing a wheel. Between us we got the wheel changed and continued on our way.

I arrived home, quite exhausted, after a ferry crossing in a gale. The Union Jack stayed in its case all the time! I lugged the thing all over Holland, it seemed, then I hauled it back to Oxford. I never did find out why I had to take it. The other English Guide, from Somerset, had to take a Union Jack to

146

*fly, somewhat easier to cope with and it was used every day
in camp. I think I drew the short straw.*

*I was just sixteen. In 1953 sixteen year olds were a lot less
sophisticated than today. It was the most enormous
adventure, the most incredible honour, not many chances of
such camps came in at that time, the selection was nation-
wide. I was over-awed by the lecture from my Captain about
being an ambassador for Guiding and for Britain. Thankfully,
she told me after the camp that I had received an excellent
report. I did not know a report would be made.*

*I had £5 pocket money for three weeks, out of that I had to get home
from London afterwards. We had help with the travelling expenses
and so on but it was an enormous expense for my family, I was one
of three and we were not well off. £5 seemed a great deal of money
to me, remember at that time £5 notes were great white things and
shop-keepers made customers sign them on the back.*

*Neither of my parents had a bank account so my Grandfather
obtained my little bit of Dutch currency.*

In 1953 a Cadet from North Oxford was presented with the
Gilt Cross Award for saving a child from death by drowning.

In the same year Miss Axtell reported to the East Oxford LA:
*The figures for the District are approximately the same as last
year but the lack of Guiders is becoming a problem.*

In January 1954 the vexed question of the partition of the City
Division was discussed. It was decided that it should remain
one Division and an Assistant Division Commissioner be
appointed. The situation would be reviewed later.

In 1955 came the perennial moan - the census money was
disgracefully high and difficult to find. It was 3/- [15p].

North Oxford District log book for 1955 mentions a Guiders'
party to be given in November by North 1 & 2:
*The Guiders decided if it was not too late to put forward the
suggestion that it would be preferable not to wear uniform at*

147

this function, Mrs Bennett agreed to see Miss Binnie [City 2 Division Commissioner] *that evening on this point.*

It was not until 1956 that the Division split, at Magdalen Bridge. Lady Rose was County Commissioner at the time and had the responsibility of it all. A coin was tossed to determine which half should be City 1 and which City 2. It was felt that Oxford North and Oxford East had social overtones that would be undesirable. The Eastern half became City 1, the Northern half, City 2. Division money was split between the new Divisions and the minutes state that

... the War Loan would be sold and divided...

It all caused some anxiety as the City had been an entity for so long and to split the City defied geography. In fact it has worked out very well, there is still a great feeling of kinship between the two Divisions but also great rivalry. The Trefoil Guild remained a City Guild, spanning the two halves.

During 1955 it was felt that the idea of Bob-a-Job week could be filched from the Scouts and so the Willing Shilling week was launched. Bob was, of course, a slang word for shilling, worth the present 5p. It was decreed that Captains would need their Commissioner's permission to hold a Willing Shilling week. At least one District have recorded their unhappiness about Guides offering their services for 1/-.

There were two Sea Rangers units within the City at this time, SRS Foudroyant and SRS Nelson. SRS Nelson met at St Mary & St John in East Oxford, SRS Foudroyant was in difficulty and it was suggested it be attached to the Girls' High School, in City 2. The Headmistress declined.

Still 1955 - there was a County Garden Party at Lady Rose's home near Reading. Two 'bus loads went from the City.

I was a very young Guider, not even warranted, when we all went to Lady Rose's. It was a beautiful day and her estate went right down to the river, it was lovely. I remember we were allowed to

roam through the house and there were unmade beds in the children's rooms. My mother came as she was in the LA and she was not pleased to see cages of white mice in the children's rooms. During 1956 it was reported that £300 was needed to re-roof the Beanwood Cottage - that was for corrugated iron to replace the thatch. It was reported later that City 1 and City 2 had contributed £70. A member of the County Cadets went to The Phillipine Islands camp.

There was a Trefoil Guild Conference in 1956, the first to be held in the Wessex area to which Oxfordshire belonged. It was held at Caxton Hall in Westminster and several delegates went from the County.

That same year 5th East Oxford Guides spent time at the Youth Hostel in Jack Straws Lane where Hungarian refugees had temporary accommodation. They peeled potatoes and washed up on Sunday mornings, the patrols taking turns. The Company was asked to make a blanket for the refugees for Christmas. Each Guide knitted four 6 inch squares and a Company meeting was occupied in stitching the blanket .

The All England Ranger Rally was held in the Albert Hall.

Still with City 1 minutes, in May 1958 it was noticed that the new second class badge test was easier and so there was a great increase in entries for proficiency badges and a consequent problem in finding testers. At that time a Guide had to gain her second class badge before entering for badges, they were proficiency badges which meant that the Guide had to show proficiency in the subject. Quite different from the present interest badges.

A Publicity Week was planned for February 1959 and the two City Divisions would co-operate. A County Rally would probably be held in 1960, Princess Margaret would be invited, our President. There would be a Youth Display with the theme of the Queen's Guide and Queen Scout badges.

5th East Oxford Guiders in camp at Saundersfoot, 1953.

In Holland, 1953, on the way to the ferry and home.

Guiders were to encourage their Guides to go on to Cadets. Cadets were in training to be Guiders, they wore white ties, white bands round their hats and white enamel badges.

Mrs Vaughan became Division Commissioner and a collection was to be made for the retiring Commissioner, Miss Hobson. It was suggested that the LA and TG be invited to contribute and a donation of 1/- was asked of Guiders [5p].

Mr Smith of the Scout Shop in Turl Street was retiring and it was suggested that he be given a Thanks Badge and a gift. After a collection had been made he was asked to choose and decided on a bird table. Mr Smith had been an institution for many years, he knew exactly what each little new Guide needed, even to the colour of her Company's tie, and he would show her how to tie the triangular tie into the correct shape. He was well loved by all of us.

City 2 invited City 1 to attend a meeting at the Taylorian Institute on St Giles addressed by Lady Burnham in December, the two Divisions were and are rivals but they co-operate and they do, contrary to rumour, still speak to each other. Seriously, the two City Divisions work together on occasions and remain good friends. Sometimes we wish we had names and not numbers but the present titles are so well known it would be pointless to change them. They roll off the tongue with great ease. Sometimes we forget that we are really <u>Oxford</u> City 1 and <u>Oxford</u> City 2.

Miss Walkinshaw, Miss Axtell and Miss Deeley leading their sub-camp at the Centenary Camp at Windsor, 1957.

Miss Axtell's certificate of attendance.

1857 B.P. 1957

M.W. Axtell .... of the

I EAST OXFORD DISTRICT Company

attended/visited the

CENTENARY·WORLD·CAMP

WINDSOR GREAT PARK

AUGUST 1957

as shown by this seal

Centenary Year

The year 1957, one hundred years after the birth of Lord Robert Baden-Powell, became the year of the Founder. A song was written in his honour, it was heady stuff:-

'... The Chief, The Chief, we thank the Lord for him ...'

A number of celebrations were planned, nationally and locally. The biggest of these was the Windsor Camp, held in Windsor Great Park. Three Guides from the County attended the camp along with Miss Walkinshaw, the County Camp's Commandant, and Miss Axtell, her QM. The camps were named after Guide homes and training centres, our camp was Our Ark, a beautiful model of an ark was suspended over the entrance. The Ark is now hanging by the entrance to Pax Lodge, Our Ark's successor in Hampstead.

There was an open day, culminating in a huge camp fire. The Princess Royal (Princess Mary), our President, was the Guest of Honour and had to apologise for not wearing her purple tie - it had been forgotten and the mistake not noticed until she changed into uniform on her 'plane.

A quote from Miss Mollie Axtell's reminiscences:

I was delighted to be on the staff and also to have my design to be the badge of the whole camp knowing that it would be carried back to all corners of the Earth.

After the camp Miss Mollie Axtell's comment was *'it was wonderful'.* She and at least one Guide went straight to their company camp from Windsor. There was a little slip-up in the organisation, the campers had days out and Mollie was included in a party to visit Oxford. She nipped home and had a bath! The County made a sampler for the camp, it went to Guides in British Guiana. Hospitality was provided in the County for campers from Leichenstein.

*1950 march-past in the Radcliffe Square, Oxford, after a Church Parade.
Miss Hobson leads City 1, Lady Rose, CC takes the salute.*

Thinking Day, 22nd February, in this Centenary year, was a particularly important date, it was, of course, The Birthday. All Guides and Guide people were encouraged to put a light, sticker or badge in a window on Thinking Day. It was reported later that very few windows were decorated, it was believed this was partly because the badges and stickers were too expensive and partly because so many Centenary events had been planned for that day. All Guides were asked to do something special on the day, City 1 and City 2 planned a World Flag on Carfax and a banner across St Aldates.

A Patrol Log from 5th East Oxford reports a District gathering:
Thinking Day, this year it is the centenary of B-P's birth on February 22nd 1857. We are celebrating this special occasion on this evening, Thursday, 21st February.

Many parents came and Miss Hobson was present, taking the chair [Division Commissioner]. *All Guides and Brownies were present and Lynn Houghton gave us a talk on her travels round the world, to the World Guide Camp in the Philippines, we had a film strip. The Guide Companies and Brownie Packs all did their pieces very well.*

The same log book from 5th East Oxford reports:
We went to the Ritz Cinema Sunday February 24th, to a Scout and Guide Thanksgiving Service for the life of Robert Baden-Powell. It was a very good service indeed.

In the evening we went to Church Parade being B-P's Centenary we chose our own hymns and lessons, the Guide Law was also said. The Service was conducted by a Minister for Headington. It was a very good service. ...

This would have been Cowley Road Methodist Church. The Company had a busy few days, as did many others. The Ritz Cinema seated 1,674 and seats had to be strictly rationed. The service was to celebrate both B-P's centenary and 50 years of Scouting. East Oxford LA Minutes records:

A unique centenary gathering of Scouts and Guides for a service in the Ritz Cinema - the largest meeting place in Oxford. [The cinema at Gloucester Green, in Oxford.]

From Professor Coulson's address:

The wonderful thing about the Scout Movement is that millions of people all over the world are trying to lead the same sort of life and abide by the same promises.

It is, of course, one of those cases where the words 'Scout Movement' are meant to include us.

On the same day the Scouts invited the Guides - over 18s - to their Founder's Day dinner on 24 February, at a cost of 10/6d [just over 50p]. This occasion was enjoyed by about 30 Guides and it was hoped the invitation would be repeated in other years. A report in the Oxford Mail indicates there were around 150 diners and quotes Mr Hazelwood, general editor for the Scout Association, as saying in his toast to Lord BP:

We must not make the mistake of building up Baden-Powell into a sort of super saint, which he wasn't. He was a good, just and likeable human being who had a good idea. The Founder was not an imaginary stuffed shirt saying wise things. He was a little man with a thousand freckles and a twinkle in his eye. He had a great sense of mischief and to him life was always exciting.

A Scout and Guide Handcraft Exhibition was planned for March as a publicity exercise in the City. It was held in the Electricity Showrooms. It was entitled EXHIBITION OF "WORKS AND TREASURES" It was opened by the Duchess of Marlborough, East Oxford District formed a Guard of Honour for the Duchess and the Mayor of Oxford.

There was to be a Ranger Rally in October but sadly, no Oxford Rangers wished to attend. An appeal for donations was made to PLs, the final County amount given was engraved on a wooden brick and given to The Chief Guide at the World Camp. City 1 collected £11 17s 0d [£11.85]. The money was for Our Ark and the World Bureau.

There was a Centenary Year Good Turn Project, the City reported the 5th East Oxford Guides raised £12 for a hospital. It seems strange they should have collected more than the City 1 Division did for the Guide appeal. Notes on Good Turns were put into a book for The Chief Guide. A Church Parade for both City Divisions was held in May to give thanks for the Founder. During the service the Guides renewed their promise after the following words from the minister:

That all may remember their high calling, let them hear the Guide Law and all renew their promise.

The Scarlet Pimpernel (5th East Oxford) log book for Thursday, 17 April 1958 records a Health item. There were 10 questions. I quote two:

8) Have you had at least one change of underclothes since last Thursday?

10) Has your Guide blouse been washed within the last month?

I was the Guider who posed those questions. It does show that some things have changed drastically. I wonder why I asked such questions anyway as it would be the mother and not the Guide who decided on clean clothes. At that time most people's washing was done by hand, put through a mangle and dried outside - everything was ironed and aired. Log books written by the Guides at this time show that spelling and English were far from perfect - a uniform berry, for instance.

In July 1958 the Royal Agricultural Show came to Kidlington and Guides were to help. We were to have a Guide Stall, a HQ stall, and we helped in other ways. City 1 was to be responsible for two Brownie displays on the 9th July. On the Tuesday 45 Guides were needed as messengers and on the

Friday 50 Guides were needed, plus 10 First Class Guides, from 8am to 5.30pm. As well as these Guiders were needed. *I remember the Royal Show at Kidlington, it was very good, we watched all the displays in the arena and we had time to go round to the stalls and to see all the animals. I was a young Guider, working on the HQ stand and I remember I was given a token for the Ladies' loo - it was a deep hole in the ground, reminded me of camp lats - not everyone had a token. My District Commissioner was there giving camp cooking displays and she was quite indignant that she had paid for this crude toilet and I had not. I lent her my token when necessary for the rest of the day. I was very tired at the end of the day but I enjoyed it. I remember Nina Phipps drove us there and back. The Show was one of the many experiences that I would not have had but for the Guides.* Later thanks were received for the Guides' contribution.

Guides from 1st Kingham joined Banbury Guides for a holiday in Austria in 1959. Beryl Jepson reported:

On the train journey out two of my Guides wanted to go to the loo, nothing unusual! Two minutes later I saw the next door carriage, where I had watched them go, being uncoupled and taken away down the line. The girls were 13 years old, spoke only English, one was my daughter and there they were, heading rapidly for the Italian border. I did not know whether to run round in circles, shout, pray, scream, collapse - in fact I froze, thinking that perhaps I would never see those girls again. I have never since experienced such utter helplessness or prayed so hard, time seemed endless - then I saw a carriage being recoupled to our train but our girls were not on it, were they really on the way to Italy? I was in despair when another carriage was connected and I could see them but all the through doors were locked and they could not reach me. The only chance was for them to get down onto the track and climb into my carriage door. I could not wait for the expected unlocking of doors just in case those carriages would be taken off again, They made it with only seconds to spare as the whole train pulled out of the station. Neither my daughter nor her companion stirred for the remainder of the journey.

In 1959 plans were laid for the Jubilee Year, 1960.

When I was married I renewed my friendship with Miss Wakelin and Miss Faint and in 1970 I returned to Guiding as a helper at St John's Brownie Pack but, of course, by the end of the year Miss Wakelin had me back in uniform.

It sounds familiar does it not?

* * * * * * * * * * * * * * * *

I was putting up wash tents, I swung my mallet - and stopped - there was a beautiful parrot perched on the tent peg. It was red and blue and spent the rest of the day in camp. We could not catch it, it had gone by morning.

Captain's birthday was on the 21st of February. It was years before I realised we were celebrating Thinking Day - I thought it was all her birthday celebrations.

We travelled to Foxlease in uniform and stopped for lunch on the way. The staff put us in a little room at the back of the restaurant although there were plenty of empty tables. As we paid we asked about our segregation and were told that Traffic Wardens were so unpopular we were not welcome. Wardens were fairly new and we did have the yellow diamonds of Brownie Guiders on our hats.

Boundary Changes

The boundary change of 1974 should be in the second history book but as we have included in this book the parts of Oxfordshire originally in Berkshire, it is recorded here.

In 1974 the whole country experienced a shock wave as Government decreed boundary changes came into force. Some counties disappeared, some were amalgamated into unhappy partnerships, Oxfordshire gained parts of Berkshire. Oxford City had always been on the edge of the county, parts of the city were in Berkshire as, to the South, the River Thames formed the boundary, now that boundary was moved. Beanwood, our only County camp site at the time, was in Berkshire. In the years since there has been much unrest about the arbitrary way the new boundaries were drawn and some decisions have been revoked. Incidentally, it is unfortunate that Oxfordshire was separated from friends in Bucks and Berks when Guiding in England was regionalised.

Oxfordshire gave a party in Rhodes House, in Oxford, for the incoming Guiders from White Horse Vale and Abingdon Divisions. The County Commissioner, Mrs Vickers, presented the two Division Commissioners with enough metal County Badges for all the Guiders. In Oxfordshire we felt an enormous relief that we were receiving newcomers and not having to move ourselves. We would not have wanted to change our badges, we felt very sorry for the Berkshire folk. The White Horse Vale Division gave us a beautiful painting of the White Horse which we planned to hang in Jubilee House when it was built. How did the Berkshire Guiders feel?

When the news broke of the intended boundary change one's immediate thought was how would this effect us all and at the same time the dread of change to our Guiding. Having a nice routine and participation as members of the Royal County of Berkshire with, perhaps, a smug view of ourselves, it was difficult to speculate as to how we would fit into a new administration. Although Guiding is universal, each County has its own independence in organisation. We know change is more difficult to accept for some people while others adapt quickly to the situation.

In July 1973 the Berkshire County Commissioner, Mrs Pepe Stratton, wrote in the County Bulletin: 'It was a very real pleasure to have with us at our AGM Mrs Gore, CC for Oxfordshire, who will be the lucky receiver of Abingdon and White Horse Vale Divisions.'

And so with trepidation we crossed the border into Oxfordshire and were given a very warm welcome. As a Trainer I was soon amalgamated into the team, somewhat daunted by the distances to travel. We had always been on the border but now looking at the map and taking in the width and length of Anglia with my name pinned with a length of thread right on the edge of the Region made me think of the challenge ahead.

Abingdon and White Horse Vale had always been very strong Divisions in Berkshire, with some forceful ladies in prominent positions, therefore it must have given Oxfordshire County Executive many topics of discussion and some headaches on how to merge the new arrivals into their system. Perhaps at first we did try to drop hints of how we used to do it, we were listened to quietly, without criticism and with a true Guiding spirit and with the welcome given by our new County we were soon working happily together.

161

NB Perhaps the saddest note was leaving our beautiful Berkshire Stag behind for the new County Badge - a cow in a puddle!

A view from an incoming Division Commissioner:
When we heard we were to leave Berkshire, where we had been so happy, I think we were all very sad. We were leaving our old friends to join up with "foreigners" - how un-Guide like! However it was soon quite clear that our fears were groundless. Mrs Gore, then CC for Oxfordshire, the County Exec and all the Guiders went to great lengths to welcome us and make the transition as easy as possible. For months before we actually joined Oxfordshire I had attended County meetings in both counties so when we finally became part of Oxon I had far less travelling to do. For me it was like coming home as I began my Guide career as a Brownie in Oxfordshire. When we were formally welcomed at a lovely ceremony at Rhodes House, we felt we were well and truly part of our new County.
Thank you Oxfordshire.

Another view:
On the whole we felt a great deal of resentment on hearing we were to be moved from Berkshire into Oxfordshire. (Who wanted an enamel cow instead of a beautiful brass stag?)
When we moved to Oxfordshire we found it very dull in the area of ceremony. No music when the Colours entered at County Do's, just the stamp of feet walking up the hall. In Berkshire the Colours were always carried to the sound of well played, well chosen music. Camping standards in Oxfordshire were far below those in Berkshire, which we felt at that time, to be the best in England. Oxfordshire did not give the Guiders the camp training or stringent licence testing we had been used to in Berkshire. We said amongst ourselves Oxfordshire campers' licences were a gift.

But we were very impressed with the friendliness of the Guiders in Oxfordshire and the wonderful welcome we received at Rhodes House. Each of us received a County badge and we learnt the Oxfordshire Vesper. After a year we found Oxfordshire had offered us a more friendly type of Guiding than Berkshire where it was very much "us and them". One seldom talked to "County" at all in Berkshire - as one Guider put it "I knows me place". It was great to be spoken to by CC, DC, etc and all treated as equals.

We soon settled in, feeling we had something to offer and something to gain. Many, when asked, say they have enjoyed their Guiding in both Counties in different ways, but then the world was changing rapidly at that time anyway.

It is hard, now, to imagine Oxfordshire bereft of White Horse Vale and Abingdon Divisions. One Guider has been heard to say she would return to Berkshire tomorrow if she could!

The earliest unit we have found in that part of Oxfordshire that moved from Berkshire is St Mary's School company, 1st White Horse, registered in 1910. In 1912 the 1st Wallingford Guide Company was opened by Miss Florence Pettit and is still an active unit. Miss Pettit was District Captain 1920-29 and belonged to a well known Wallingford family. In 1918 1st and 2nd Wantage Guides were formed.

The next year, 1919, 1st Moulsford Company camped at Upper Basildon with 1st Warborough, an Oxfordshire company. It seems that there was co-operation between Oxfordshire and Berkshire even then.

In 1922 the 1st Chosley Guides and Brownies opened and although they have been closed and re-opened through the years they are both open and alive today. 1923 saw the 1st Moulsford Guides camping at Niton, in the Isle of Wight, with the 8th Oxford Guides - more co-operation!

In 1926 Wallingford District Rally, arranged for 15th May, was cancelled at short notice because of the General Strike.

The 1st Didcot Guides opened in 1927.

The 1st Moulsford Guide camp in the New Forest was cancelled in 1929 due to an outbreak of smallpox, strict vaccination orders were in force.

In 1939 the 1st Didcot Guides lost both their Captain and Lieutenant to the ATS along with two Didcot Rangers. That year the District Ranger Company opened in Didcot and the small 1st Wallingford Ranger Company opted to join the District unit. During the war the 1st Didcot Guides knitted blanket squares for military hospitals and collected used stamps, silver foil and grew potatoes. (We still collect stamps and foil in the nineties, for Jubilee House.)

We are aware, of course, that other activities took place in this area and that other units helped the war effort.

The original North Berkshire Division became Abingdon Division and two Districts were transferred to White Horse Vale when it was formed. Didcot was separated from Wallingford in 1969 and in 1977 was split into Didcot and Didcot Downs District to form, with Wallingford, Ridge Way Division. The split in Didcot was not popular and in 1983 they were re-united.

* * * * * * * * * * * * * * * *

Please note, only Oxfordshire Guides are allowed to refer to our County Badge as a cow-in-a-puddle!

We always wore our Guide uniform to school on Thinking Day and Empire Day. I wore my Guide badge in my school tie all through senior school. It ruined my tie.

Jubilee Year, 1960

A brief look at Jubilee Year - the next book will start here.

1960 - fifty years old and still going as strong or stronger than ever. Plans to celebrate this milestone were laid in 1959. These notes are taken from City 1 minutes.

A County Rally was planned. A County camp was to be at Ditchley Park 26th July - 2nd August. Lady Baden-Powell was to be invited to visit. By this time The Chief Guide was an old lady, still travelling the world on our behalf but becoming frail. She lived in a Grace and Favour apartment at Hampton Court and was highly respected - not only by Guides and Scouts.

A National Celebration at Wembley was planned in which 24 Oxfordshire Guides would take part.

Thinking Day would see a Gathering at the Oxford Town Hall. There would be Brownie Revels at Temple Cowley School on the 28th May, the LAs would be asked to help. A campfire and fireworks were planned for Beanwood. Three Guides would attend the Church services in London. The Chief Guide would be invited to a dinner in Banbury. A souvenir card was to be given to Guides and Brownies. Miss Axtell designed this. A church parade would be held on 29th May, with a tea party to follow.

Alas, not all these plans came to fruition.

It was decided not to hold a Rally and it was suggested that South Park would be a better venue for the campfire. It was reported later that eight Guides from the County went to Wembley, two of them from City 1. Two Guides, one Guider and one Sea Ranger went from City 1 to the Jubilee Service in London. Headington School offered to host the campfire in the school grounds. The Brownie Revels would not take

Above: *The special badge designed by Miss Mollie Axtell.*

Below: *At the Oxford Camp at Ditchley to celebrate the Golden Jubilee of Guiding, 1960.*

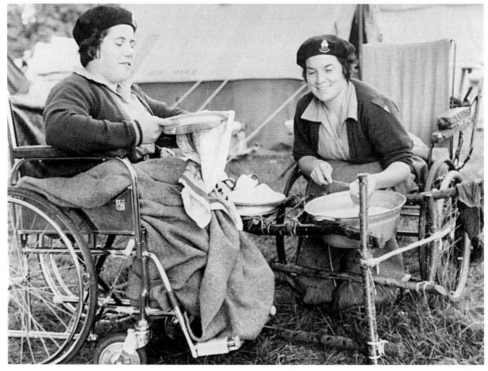

place if the weather was unsuitably wet.

Some plans worked very well - the Thinking Day celebration for example - the Oxford Mail reported that more than 600 girls from 24 companies attended the celebrations in Oxford's Town Hall.

The celebrations were attended by a large number of parents and friends. The guest of honour was the Mayor. ... The international aspect of Guiding was stressed throughout the evening.

The police were informed of the expected influx of Guides. It was later agreed that the occasion had been a big success.

The Jubilee Camp Fire was conducted by Miss Axtell. Districts were to provide cardboard boxes to collect ice cream papers. The Scarlet Pimpernel Patrol (5th East Oxford) log book records the camp fire in Headington School grounds on Saturday, 29th June 1960.

... We had an interval in which we were given ice creams. after more songs we were given a souvenir card designed by Hawk. Many kind fathers had supplied fireworks and after these came 'Taps' and Oxford Vesper.

[Hawk was Miss Mollie Axtell's camp name.]

At this time the Company was earning and collecting money for the Mayor of Oxford's Refugee Fund.

In 1960, to celebrate 50 years of Guiding, a large County camp was organised at Ditchley Park. Betty, daughter of Lord and Lady Baden-Powell visited the camp, visitors' day was held in pouring rain.

The Wembley Festival produced a profit of £7,000. Remember, this was in 1960. Joy Markly was to go to the International Camp in Canada.

The year ended with Mrs Vaughan, City 1 Division Commissioner representing the Division at the Town Hall for the Queen's visit.

I remember seeing Miss Walkinshaw's dog running round Beanwood with a plastic mug stuck over its muzzle. The dog went everywhere with her and on this occasion had been trying to lick out a mug.

Hawk was strict about the camp kitchen. I remember a visitor, one of her Guides from years ago, at camp with two young daughters. The younger child was 'helping' us get the tea and she licked her fingers. Hawk, very gently, took her away from the kitchen area. [Hawk was Miss Axtell.]

Beanwood was overbooked. I remember one camp on the cottage side of the big tree and one on the other side.

We made an altar out of boxes of vegetables, mainly lettuce, The visiting minister, the Reverend Rimmer, noticed this and we were hard put to keep straight faces as he intoned "Lettuce pray".

I love Beanwood, we all learnt to camp there and I have so many happy memories of the camps.

. . . and Finally

When those first intrepid girls started their Guiding in Oxfordshire, they could not have envisaged the momentous legacy that they would create. The number of girls and women whose lives have been touched and, in some cases, dramatically changed by their involvement in Guiding must be tremendous. Some would have joined for a short while; some would be totally committed for a lifetime, but all would have memories, friends and a standard to live up to that came from their time in Guiding.

Guiding in Oxfordshire has continually grown over the years and although trends have changed the structure and programme to make sure they are up-to-date, the Guiding Principles have never diminished. The Promise and Law are still at the heart of everything we do, as is the commitment of providing opportunities for girls and women to achieve their potential.

The story does not end here, the legacy continues and many more girls and women have still to be involved, to create memories and to make friends all over the world as well as in Oxfordshire, through Guiding.

Evelyn Walker
County Commissioner

1999.